THE APU TRILOGY

Contemporary Approaches
to Film and Media Series

GENERAL EDITOR

Barry Keith Grant, Brock University

ADVISORY EDITORS

Robert J. Burgoyne, University of St. Andrews

Caren J. Deming, University of Arizona

Patricia B. Erens, School of the Art Institute of Chicago

Peter X. Feng, University of Delaware

Lucy Fischer, University of Pittsburgh

Frances Gateward, California State University, Northridge

Tom Gunning, University of Chicago

Thomas Leitch, University of Delaware

Walter Metz, Southern Illinois University

A complete listing of the books in this series
can be found online at wsupress.wayne.edu

NEW EDITION

THE APU TRILOGY

ROBIN WOOD

EDITED BY BARRY KEITH GRANT
PREFACE BY RICHARD LIPPE

WAYNE STATE UNIVERSITY PRESS
DETROIT

© 2016 by Wayne State University Press, Detroit, Michigan 48201.
All rights reserved. No part of this book may be reproduced
without formal permission.
Manufactured in the United States of America.

20 19 18 17 16   5 4 3 2 1

Library of Congress Cataloging Number: 2016941895

ISBN 978-0-8143-3277-1 (paperback)
ISBN 978-0-8143-4226-8 (ebook)

Designed and typeset by Bryce Schimanski
Composed in Adobe Caslon Pro

Wayne State University Press
Leonard N. Simons Building
4809 Woodward Avenue
Detroit, Michigan 48201-1309

Visit us online at wsupress.wayne.edu

CONTENTS

Foreword by Barry Keith Grant vii
Preface by Richard Lippe xi

Introduction *1*
Pather Panchali 25
Aparajito 55
The World of Apu 79

Notes *127*
Filmography *129*
Index *145*

FOREWORD
BARRY KEITH GRANT

The Apu Trilogy is the fifth book by the influential film critic Robin Wood to be republished by Wayne State University Press within its Contemporary Approaches to Film and Media Series. It follows the updated *Howard Hawks* (2006) and the expanded monographs *Ingmar Bergman* (2013) and *Arthur Penn* (2014), three of Wood's early and pioneering auteurist studies originally published in the 1960s, and *Personal Views* (2006), a collection of essays previously published in 1976 only in the United Kingdom. *Personal Views*, like *Ingmar Bergman* and *Arthur Penn*, was significantly expanded with other, later essays by Wood included in the new editions. The book on Hawks, however, was published unchanged except for a new introduction by Wood because, as he wrote there, "Of all my early books . . . this is the one that seems to me to require the least qualification and/or apology." Wood's admiration for and interest in Hawks was unwavering because, while his views of Bergman and Alfred Hitchcock (the subject of another early directorial study already revisited by the author) evolved substantially as his criticism became more politically aware, his opinion of Hawks remained largely unchanged. "Hawks remains Hawks," as Wood asserted.

The Apu Trilogy, like the Hawks book, is republished here in its original form, although not necessarily because Wood's thinking about the director Satyajit Ray's work, including the trilogy, remained unchanged over the intervening decades. As Richard Lippe, Wood's partner of many years, explains in his preface, it was Wood's intention to revise the book, but, alas, poor health prevented him from ever doing so. And although Wood wrote little about Ray subsequently, we know that Ray remained an important filmmaker for him given his unfulfilled wish late in his life to revise it.

That Ray's films were of great significance for Wood is amply demonstrated by this relatively slim volume on the Apu trilogy. Of Wood's early monographs, it is the only one to focus on a few specific films rather than a filmmaker's entire career up to the point of writing. The book's subject may have been the least familiar to North American readers at the time, but it is also the most sustained critical commentary that this remarkably insightful and eloquent critic ever produced. Focusing on only three films—*Pather Panchali* (1955), *Aparajito* (*The Unvanquished*, 1957), and *Apu Sansar* (*The World of Apu*, 1959), all of which follow the character of Apu Roy as he grows from a boy to adulthood—from Ray's prolific career, which included directing more than two dozen features as well as several shorts and documentary films and composing the music for almost all of them, Wood demonstrates more clearly here than anywhere his ability at detailed textual analysis, providing an impressively sustained reading of these three films that demonstrates their worthiness to be regarded as among the major achievements of world cinema.

FOREWORD

Wood was one of the most insightful and committed advocates of an authentically humanistic cinema. Despite his increasingly politicized perspective, he championed films that explore the human condition (in *Personal Views*, he unapologetically refers to himself as an "unreconstructed humanist"), and his analysis of the Apu trilogy reveals and illuminates the films' profoundly humanistic qualities with exemplary clarity and rigor, plumbing the psychological and emotional resonances that arise from Ray's delicate balance of performance, camera work, and visual design. Wood demonstrates his mastery of close textual reading without being blind to what he regards as the films' flaws. If some scenes seem to him forced or contrived, in discussing others he identifies the profound interconnectedness of life and death that Ray captures in the trilogy and so demonstrates their aesthetic value. Lippe's affecting account of the director's visit with Wood reveals Ray's appreciation for the regard in which Wood held his work.

As has been the case with all of Wood's film books republished by Wayne State University Press, the aim here has been to preserve not only the original text but also the format and look of the books as much as possible. In the case of the present book, almost all of the images in the original that were frame captures have been retained; but the reverse printing of several of them has been corrected, and those that suffered cropping have had their proper frames restored. The support of Annie Martin, senior acquisitions editor at the press, and the entire editorial board and staff has made this book's publication, along with the earlier reprints of Wood's books, possible and is here gratefully acknowledged. I should also like to thank Chris Thomas, honorary secretary of the Powys Society, for promptly tracking down the quotation from T. F. Powys's novel *Unclay*. Once again, Rob Macmorine and Dan Barnowski of Brock University provided invaluable technical assistance.

Wood's early auteurist studies were extraordinarily influential when first published. I have commented in the earlier monographs on the historical significance of these books, but it bears repeating that during a period when few reviewers and critics were taking film criticism seriously, Wood's careful and thoroughly cinematic commentaries demonstrated the potential of film analysis in a nascent scholarly field. Of course, other critics already had written about Hawks, Hitchcock, Bergman, and Penn before Wood, although none with the same degree of insight or influence. But Wood was the first English-language critic to write substantively about Ray's films, which made the original publication of his monograph on the Apu trilogy unprecedented as well as impressive. Of late, there has been a renewed interest in North America in the work of Satyajit Ray, yet no other critic has come close to equaling the scope and depth of Wood's analysis.

PREFACE
RICHARD LIPPE

After Robin Wood committed himself to the Wayne State University Press offer to update the directorial monographs, he initially thought of working on the Bergman book, but he rejected the idea after considering the number of films that had followed *Shame* (1968). Furthermore, he felt his occasional writings on Bergman through the years had made clear his reconsidered position on the director. Instead, Robin chose to write on Satyajit Ray's work, much of which he hadn't seen in years. The neglect didn't mean he no longer valued Ray. During the early '70s he was confronted with new critical tools and the introduction of film theory; in addition, he began to direct his energy to writing on the contemporary American horror film, with its subversive potential to critique the dominant ideology, and on the directors of these films. Moreover, it was difficult to see sixteen-millimeter prints of Ray's films, which received poor distribution. The situation improved somewhat with the introduction of VHS and later DVDs.

In preparing to work on the project, Robin collected sixteen films, aside from the trilogy, from various periods of Ray's career. His response after watching several of them was a delight in their excellence and in reestablishing a connection with Ray. The films gave him a lot of pleasure, and undoubtedly he would have written a series of exceptional essays. Robin saw his updating of the book as a means to stimulate interest in this long overlooked and undervalued director. Unfortunately, his health was rapidly declining, and he never managed to write on any of the films. If Robin were alive now, he would be thankful for Criterion's release of the Apu trilogy and the attention it will surely draw to Ray and his films.

The Apu Trilogy was published in 1971 and is the final monograph Robin wrote. *Pather Panchali*, *Aparajito*, and *The World of Apu* were released between 1955 and 1959. Robin says in his introduction that Ray was then treated with critical indifference or, as was typical with his colleagues at *Movie*, with a perfunctory respect. In response, he offers possible reasons why this occurred, including social and cultural differences and the films' slow pacing, which contemporary critics tended to associate with classical cinema. Robin went on to counter these superficial justifications for dismissing Ray. He mentions Ray's admiration for Western film culture, including the Hollywood cinema and European directors, particularly Jean Renoir and his realist films. In effect, his opening comments are not dissimilar from the question that opens his Hitchcock book: "Why should we take Hitchcock seriously?" (*Hitchcock's Films*, 1965). In the case of Hitchcock, the issue was that the director was perceived critically as an entertainer and not as an artist;

with Ray, the critical contention was his "otherness." Robin's position was that Ray dealt with primal concerns, such as "birth, death, marriage, the family, parenthood," that are universal and readily accessible to all. Furthermore, as he notes, Ray's films deal with emotions, not concepts, allowing the viewer to relate to the narratives more directly.

In regard to the monographs, it is noteworthy that Robin's commitment to Bergman was also based on "universals" and emotional response. In Bergman's films, these concerns tend to be centered on gender/sex conflicts that are explored in a context involving isolation and some degree of abstraction. Robin's disenchantment with Bergman began with his realization that the director's "universal condition" was grounded in an ideological worldview that he took for lived reality. In addition, Bergman, when confronted, maintained his vision as "truth," as Robin says in his essay "From the Lives of the Marionettes: Bergman, Sweden and Me" (*Ingmar Bergman*, 2013). Bergman wasn't a "political" filmmaker, and he didn't accept ideology as a societal factor; instead, he privileged alienation and a psychoanalytic interpretation of human behavior.

Arguably, Ray wasn't politically inclined either. Nevertheless, Robin stresses throughout *The Apu Trilogy* that the characters are significantly shaped by their background, environment, and socioeconomic conditions. During the course of a narrative, a character may progressively evolve, as does Apu, who seeks education and knowledge to develop, or not, as in the case of his mother, Sarbojaya, who clings to tradition and to her role as wife and mother. In that capacity, her behavior is frequently harsh because of her disempowerment and her concern with her image as a parent among women better off. As a critic in the late '60s, Robin may not have fully comprehended the concept of ideological criticism, but he was sensitive to the underlying political grounding of the trilogy. Ray's humanism found its counterpart in Robin's responsiveness to the director's films. And like Ray, Robin was concerned with the reasons that account for an individual's identity—a concern that ideological critics dismissed as irrelevant.

One of the aspects of this book that is particularly rewarding is Robin's analytical approach to the trilogy and the other Ray films he discusses. Robin, with the introduction and the three essays, offers an excellent account of evaluative criticism. He is consistently clear about his methodology and its application. He argues why the films deserve detailed attention both on an individual basis and as a trilogy and goes on to illustrate his contentions through rigorous readings. The book functions as a master class on what constitutes an in-depth reading of a work and the use of critical tools that are relevant to the undertaking. Robin places himself at the service of the films to make his assessment, not through an application of preconceived theoretical notions.

I would like to refer briefly to the three essays and Robin's critical approach to each. To begin, *Pather Panchali*, in dealing with the Roy family, features five major interrelating characters. Although Hari, the father, is frequently absent, he is nevertheless a significant character as Apu inherits his intellectual nature. In his absence, Sarbojaya is forced to be both a mother and a father figure, and Apu's closest ties are to his mother and older sister, Durga. The fifth crucial character is Auntie, an aged relative who lives with them. Through a discussion of mise-en-scène and editing, Robin elaborates on the layers of meaning found within these characters and on the narrative's movement. His analysis of the sequence in which Durga and Apu have their first experience of seeing a train as it hurtles through an open field and its juxtaposition with Auntie's death is exceptionally eloquent. Using descriptive imagery, Robin manages to communicate the force of Ray's visual poetry in this meditation on youth and age. This is also evident in his delicate discussion of Auntie and her death. Auntie, in her at times defiant and self-centered struggle to care for herself and justify her existence, is the film's (and the trilogy's) most troubling and disturbing presence. Robin doesn't extract the character to make a statement on primitive culture, poverty, or ageism but respects Ray's presentation of her. The character warrants compassion, and Ray provides it, as Robin illustrates, through a close observation of the scenes and their stylistics.

Of the three films, Robin finds *Aparajito* to be the most schematic in pointing to how personal and geographical distance affects Sarbojaya and Apu's relationship after Hari's death. In calling attention to Ray's structural approach, Robin isn't merely making note of a formal device. Rather, he points to the significance the director places on a character's desires and emotional needs. Sarbojaya gradually realizes that Apu is drifting away from her as he pursues an education in a contemporary world that is alien to her. Apu is less conscious of what is happening between them, but his conflicting responses to his mother's behavior suggest a rejection of her emotional disposition. The situation itself is a familiar one that is inevitable in many parent-child relationships.

Ray structures the middle film as a series of increasingly awkward encounters between mother and son that build to a communication breakdown, which is followed by Sarbojaya's death. Ray documents this intimate and painful experience and does so without judging either of the characters. In *Aparajito*, he emphatically dramatizes the fragility and complexities of familial relations.

The essay on *The World of Apu* is the longest and most detailed of the three. Ray made two films—*The Philosopher's Stone* and *The Music Room*—between *Aparajito* and *The World of Apu*, and Robin argues that Ray grew as a filmmaker during that time. In *The World of Apu*, Apu is now a young adult on his own; the film traces the stages of his development, culminating in the death of his wife while giving birth to their son and his rejection of the child, whom he blames for her death. His maturity occurs when he accepts his young son and regains his will to live. Robin implicitly suggests that the narrative mirrors Ray's own maturing as an artist. Robin's critical approach to the film is to point to the nuances, whether in characterization or stylistics, that Ray brings to each step of Apu's experience and growth. The essay is comparable to the *Pather Panchali* piece in its emphasis on how unforeseen change occurs and, in turn, affects future choices. In *The World of Apu*, the difference is that Apu is an intellectual, and the devastating death of his wife causes a response akin to an existential crisis. For Robin, it stands as one of Ray's finest achievements and, organically, completes the trilogy that essentially begins with Apu's birth.

Around the time Robin was writing *The Apu Trilogy*, he got to meet Ray, who happened to be in England on a visit. According to Robin's ex-wife, Aline, Robin and Ray met at the

Hilton Hotel in London. I remember Robin telling me about a meeting with Ray that took place at his home. He said that on a Sunday morning the doorbell rang, and when he opened the door, much to his surprise and delight, Ray was standing there smiling and said he had decided to drop by and say hello. Robin said he liked Ray a lot. While Robin doesn't mention his meeting with Ray in the book, he does say in discussing *The World of Apu*, "The finest qualities of Ray's characters are those perceptible in his own films: while watching them, one feels in the presence of an exceptionally kind, generous, warm, and sympathetic human being." Perhaps these sentiments were reinforced after meeting with Ray.

I recall also Robin saying he had mentioned to Ray how much he enjoyed Blake Edwards's *The Party* (1968) and Peter Sellers's performance as the bumbling protagonist. Immediately after saying it, Robin began thinking the comment might have been improper or even offensive. Instead, Ray's response was that he too thought the film and Sellers were hilarious!

In June 2010, Piers Handling and Steve Gravestock of the TIFF/Toronto International Film Festival mounted a ten-film tribute to Robin. They invited me to participate in selecting the films. Our choices were director orientated, with the priority being directors whom Robin particularly valued and who were relevant to his critical writings. Of course, Hitchcock, Hawks, Bergman, and Penn were included, as was Satyajit Ray. The Ray film we screened was *Days and Nights in the Forest* (1969), which Robin considered to be one of Ray's most accomplished works. (Because of the ten-film format, a screening of the trilogy wouldn't have been feasible.)

PREFACE

Although *The Apu Trilogy* is a slim volume, it is essential reading for anyone who values Robin as a critic. The book is also an indispensable introduction to Ray's best known and most revered films. I thank Wayne State University Press for making *The Apu Trilogy* available to contemporary readers.

INTRODUCTION

One likes to begin a book with a bit of controversy, punching a few critical noses and offering one's own for the return poke or smash that all too seldom comes. The reader always enjoys finding a few insults bandied around: aside from the dubious pleasure of sharing in a probably quite unjustified feeling of superiority, it gives one the sense that there must be some issue at stake, for one to make up one's own mind about. Alas, in the case of Satyajit Ray, it is next to impossible to achieve this desirable effect: there seems never to have been any controversy about him.

This certainly does not mean that there is uniformity of opinion about the value of Ray's work: the critics with whom my own name has most often been linked, the founders and authors of *Movie*, reject him to a man. But then "reject" is altogether too strong a word. Rather, they offer him the insult that is beyond insult: they ignore him. One once told me that *Pather Panchali* "seemed quite a nice little film," which seems to be about the maximum enthusiasm Ray's films have aroused in those quarters. Critics who detest Jean-Luc Godard and Ingmar Bergman usually find them sufficiently interesting and stimulating to be worth the bother of attacking, but Ray appears to provoke in his detractors nothing more intense than apathy. Whereas most of Godard's detractors wouldn't dream of missing a new Godard film, there is a general sense among Ray's that *Mahanagar* and *Charulata* wouldn't be worth the time and bus fare. The corollary is that Ray's admirers (in print at least) tend to be critics of the conservative Establishment. Film enthusiasts who don't know Ray's work well at first hand probably build up a mental image of it as the sort of primitive and literary cinema that has a solid, dull worthiness but is difficult spontaneously to enjoy or get excited about.

I propose to begin by attempting to do the detractors' work for them: to elaborate, out of the shrug of indifference that is the most those who are hostile to his work seem willing to offer, a case against Ray (in order, naturally, to refute it)—to imagine, that is, the obstacles that interfere with other people's response to films that have always communicated very directly and movingly to *me*.

First, perhaps, I should confront the problem—which, confronted, appears more hypothetical than real—of the accessibility of Ray's films for Western audiences: can we feel any confidence that we are adequately understanding, intellectually and emotionally, works that are the product of a culture very different from our own? The problem has two aspects. One is content, our intermittent sense that certain passages or details in the films may mean something more, or something different, to Indian audiences. The other is tempo: the chief explicit grumble in the West about Ray's films is that they move slowly.

The "content" problem can easily be stood on its head: what is remarkable is how *seldom* in Ray's films the spectator is pulled up by any specific obstacle arising from cultural differences. Partly, this can be attributed to the fact that Ray appears to have learned his art mainly from the Western cinema. The directors he repeatedly refers to, as antecedents rather than direct influences, are Jean Renoir (*The Southerner*, *The River*), Vittorio De Sica (*Bicycle Thieves*), John Ford, and Frank Capra; he has expressed admiration for directors as diverse as Ingmar Bergman and Alfred Hitchcock. In terms of general subject matter, Ray's films usually deal with human fundamentals that undercut all cultural distinctions. The subject matter of the trilogy—family, the parent-child relationship, marriage, irreparable loss, reconciliation—is obviously universal in its accessibility. Even Ray's apparently more "exotic" films like *Devi*—in which a young girl is mistaken by her father-in-law for a reincarnation of a goddess—can be reduced to conflicts (usually related to social change and the gulf between generations) that are certainly not restricted to one culture. When a specific cultural peculiarity *does* play a part in the narrative, it often becomes evident that the attitude to it encouraged by the film as a whole is not all that far removed from our own. The impromptu wedding in *The World of Apu* is a case in point. We no longer arrange marriages for our daughters with men they have never met, and even if we did and the groom, on arrival, proved to be insane, we would not assume that the girl was cursed and perennially unmarriageable if a substitute were not found at once to go through with the ceremony. But the consciousness through which we view all this is Apu's, and his immediate reaction is "Are we still living in the Dark Ages?" Similarly, in *Devi*, the attitude we are encouraged to identify with most closely is that of the horrified young husband: the superstition is seen unequivocally as that and as monstrous.

The "tempo" problem presents more serious obstacles; it is also much more difficult to discuss or remove, depending as it does partly on subjective reaction and on aspects of film that it is impossible to cope with at all adequately in words. Even making allowances for possible national differences in expectation, there are passages in Ray that I feel to be "stretched": within the trilogy, the later sequences of *Aparajito* (*Teen Kanya*); outside it, the later scenes of the second story of *Two Daughters*. In both these cases, we see where the film is moving long before it gets there and feel we would accept a more elliptical treatment than Ray's painstaking analysis of each phase in the development of character and narrative. Even here, however, we should be ready to allow for the fact that Ray is less interested in expressing ideas than in communicating emotional experience. In the West, we are conditioned primarily either by the classic American cinema, with its taut narrative structures in which, when a scene has made its point, we are carried swiftly on to the next, or by the European "art" cinema, with its tendency to intellectual thematic structures. We may feel, with Ray, that we have already got the point when we are in fact continuing to miss it, for "the point" may be not an extractable thematic or narrative issue but the total experience a character is undergoing.

More generally, the only answer to the complaint that Ray's films move "slowly" is that this is surely their right. Rules cannot be applied externally to works of art, for each work defines its own rules. To ask Ray's films to move faster is like asking Brahms or Bruckner to be Stravinsky. This is not to say that either Brahms or Bruckner (or Ray) is necessarily beyond criticism, but the right to criticize is earned only by submitting to the work in question sufficiently to feel its movement, its rhythms, its breathing. Only

INTRODUCTION

then can we decide with any degree of authority whether or not a point is being labored; the criterion is not the tempo adopted but our sense of the artist's success in realizing his or her concepts and, ultimately, the value of the concepts as realized.

In fact, Ray has himself stated unequivocally that the best critical writings on his films have appeared in the West.[1] Certainly any diffidence about discussing films that the very different cultural background may lead one partly to misconstrue is best dispelled by turning to the critical work of some of Ray's fellow countrymen. A Bombay magazine called *Montage* devoted an entire issue to Ray's work. It constitutes a valuable document, though not entirely because of the quality of its contents, which is, to say the least, variable. Most interesting, in fact, apart from Ray's own contributions in interviews and articles, are the interviews with his collaborators, both actors and technicians. The critical articles are not uniformly undistinguished, but the level of some of them might well encourage the hesitant Western critic to feel that cultural differences do not necessarily disqualify him or her from attempting to analyze Ray's work responsibly. An article titled "Death in the Trilogy" by T. G. Vaidyanathan, for instance, offers this account of a scene closely following the announcement of Aparna's death in *The World of Apu*: "as Apu is preparing to leave and crosses the railway tracks, he notices a white goat while simultaneously discerning the approach of a train. The train emits a long whistle as it approaches, and on nearing Apu, the camera veers skyward and the blankness of the empty sky envelops us as the long deepening screech of the whistle takes the train past Apu. The white goat is almost certainly run over."[2] We might charitably forgive the curious substitution of a "white goat" for the film's quite unambiguous pig, as a lapse of memory; but so striking a lapse does rather undermine any faith in the accuracy of the rest of the description, offered with such a confident show of detail. And why "is almost certainly run over"? We see the animal dead! The sequence in fact *begins* with the empty sky and the smoke; Apu notices the pig only when he hears its death scream. But the really startling omission is the writer's total lack of awareness of what the staging, acting, and editing of the scene make clear beyond any shadow of a doubt: that Apu, as he awaits the train's arrival, is contemplating suicide; that it is only the pig's death that prevents him from casting himself under the train. The next essay in the *Montage* issue, "The Theme of Love in Ray's Films," by Goutam Kaul, offers an even more remarkable distortion, and with reference to a film whose subject matter might well occasion the Western critic some qualms. The subject of *Devi*, according to Kaul, is "a man's growing awareness that his wife was a goddess incarnate." I don't see how anyone— Eskimo, Hottentot, or Anthropophagus—who attended at all to the film could make *that* of it. Obviously, it would be rash, from such meager evidence, to jump to the conclusion that Ray's films are understood *better* by Westerners than by his compatriots; but at least it is an encouragement to overcome any natural diffidence and sense of disadvantage.

By aligning Ray, in my rough-and-ready analogy, with Brahms and Bruckner against Stravinsky, I may have seemed to concede the detractors' strongest point: Ray is, after all, a twentieth-century artist—isn't his cinema desperately old-fashioned? To which one can imagine the hypothetical detractor adding, as an afterthought, the dread words "literary" and "academic." The emergence in the

INTRODUCTION

West of Ray's early work preceded by a few years the breaking of the New Wave and English-speaking critics' discovery of Antonioni. The quiet and undemonstrative qualities of *Pather Panchali* of course never generated the sort of excitement associated with early Godard. By the time *The World of Apu* was released in London, it could have been seen sandwiched between *L'Avventura* the day before and *Les Bonnes Femmes* the day after, in which context, with no allowances for the artistic and social environment from which it came, it must have certainly appeared old-fashioned. But not to make such allowances is manifestly absurd, and to call *Pather Panchali* old-fashioned in relation to *L'Avventura* is as meaningless as to call *Broken Blossoms* old-fashioned beside *Breathless*: of course it is, and the label does not reduce the film's value in the slightest. It is easy to guess that, in the context of the Bengali cinema, *Pather Panchali* was positively revolutionary. Ray's models were Renoir and the Italian neorealists, but "models" isn't really the right term because Ray's film does not in any real sense imitate them; rather, they gave Ray the kind of hints a great artist can take from others and use in his or her own way. It is true that Ray has not obviously extended the boundaries of cinematic expression, except perhaps in the context of Indian cinema; he is naturally conservative by temperament. But the same could be said of Ford and Hawks and even of Renoir and Mizoguchi. Other directors can learn from all of these abundantly, as they can from Ray, but none has been responsible for the kind of startling, instantly transforming innovations one associates with *Citizen Kane* or *Breathless*. Ray hasn't been afraid to adopt the innovations of others when they suit his purposes (the use of the zoom lens and "freeze" shots in *Charulata*, for example), but on the whole, he has shown himself content with the filmmaker's traditional means and methods, which he has turned to consistently personal use. The term "academic" only has force if it implies a characterless following of rules, the safe reliance on repetition of what has been done before. Analysis will show, I think, that the decisions one can discern through Ray's mise-en-scène nearly always grow out of a personal response to the material. Nor is Ray in any real sense a "primitive," as my analogy with D. W. Griffith's *Broken Blossoms* may have misleadingly suggested. The sensibility with which one makes contact through the films is notably refined and civilized, and the technique, within the limits of "classical" mise-en-scène (a term I take to include Mizoguchi and Renoir, so the limits are not exactly constricting), has a corresponding delicacy.

The charge of Ray's cinema being "literary" might seem to carry rather more weight. Most of his films are adapted from novels and stories, and most of the originals have the reputation of being respectable, distinguished works in their own right. His art clearly has affinities with that of the novelist, his most obvious concern being with the nuances of character relationships and character development. Yet careful examination of almost any sequence in Ray's work will show that it has been conceived—or, when the literary original is closely followed, reconceived—in terms that are essentially cinematic. This holds true even of simple dialogue scenes taking place within a single set: camera position, camera movement, and editing are not mere functional appendages but play a leading creative role, so that the overall effect is not only nonliterary but nontheatrical.

At this point, it might be useful to support these assertions with an example—which, as the Apu films will be discussed in

INTRODUCTION

detail later, I shall take from one of Ray's later works. Consider, then—as a representative specimen, the rule rather than the exception—a scene from the first story of *Two Daughters*. The story (the original is by Tagore) is about an educated young man from the city who gets the job of postmaster in a primitive rural village. With the job, he inherits from his predecessor a small orphan girl called Ratan, whose duties include cleaning the house and driving away the local lunatic. Without family or guardians, Ratan begins to develop an attachment to the young man, taking very much to heart his remarks about cleanliness and domestic efficiency. Just before the sequence in question, we see her taking off the line her clothes, diligently washed to please him. There follows a scene organized by Ray into thirteen shots: (1) The all-purpose living room in the postmaster's house. He is lying on his stomach on the bed in very grubby clothes, face toward the camera, looking at a postcard, holding an open book. The camera is sufficiently far back to reveal much of the décor: the family photograph the postmaster has put on the wall, left; the umbrella he carries everywhere with him, emblem of his importance, hanging on the wall. The background of the shot is sunlit. The young man's face suggests a quiet happiness. Just before Ratan enters in the background, the camera tracks in, so that the two figures are framed more tightly. She speaks; he slips the postcard into the book and turns on his back. (2) A medium shot of Ratan, standing against the window. She pauses, expectant: she wants him to notice her clean clothing. Then she asks him who the letter is from. The postmaster (outside the image) tells her it's from his mother. She smiles. (3) The postmaster: "Why do you smile?" (4) Ratan. She runs left to the photo on the wall, triumphantly pointing out the figure she has deduced (correctly) to be his mother. The camera first follows Ratan left, then tracks back to take in the young man as well, as Ratan points to another figure and asks who she is. "My sister Rani," he tells her. (5) Close-up, Ratan. She looks troubled. "Can she read and write?" (6) The postmaster has turned his back on her and is lying on his side. We see him from her point of view. "And sing too," he says. (7) Ratan again. The young man's voice continues: "She's not like you." "But I can sing," the child promptly answers. (8) The postmaster's back. Ratan's voice: "Shall I show you?" (9) Ratan begins to sing, nervously fingering her sari, looking down at the floor. The camera tracks back to show the postmaster apparently asleep, then tracks in to a close-up of him to show his eyes opening as the hesitant song continues. (10) Ratan fingering the sari, singing. She stops. "That's all I know." (11) The postmaster, close-up. He laughs. "It was very good." The camera tracks back to take in Ratan. He goes on to tell her she must learn to read and write too—then she'll be like his sister. He tells her to look for money in his coat pocket, to buy a slate and pencil. The camera tracks in slightly as he gives her some of the money she brings him. "I only need eight pennies," she says. (12) The postmaster: "Keep the rest. If you study hard." (13) A shot of them both. His voice continues: "and you'll get more." Ratan runs out of frame right, then comes back and pauses again. "Oh," he says, noticing at last, "you've washed your clothes."

Acting is one of the aspects of film least susceptible to verbal analysis, but it must be said that much of the scene's delicate and touching quality arises from the precision and sensitivity of the performances, the man's casual indifference, then faint stirring of interest contrasted with the child's shy eagerness to please (Ray is arguably the cinema's greatest director of children). And it is real *film* acting, much too delicately nuanced to make an effect from a stage. What can be pointed out more satisfactorily is the way Ray uses the purely cinematic means of camera movement and editing to express the essence of the scene: the sense of hesitant contact. The device of cutting not with the dialogue but in counterpoint to it, so that one character's words are combined with the other's reaction to them, is not just a means of achieving greater fluidity in the editing. In (7), for example, the effect of juxtaposing the young man's words "She's not like you" with a shot of Ratan is greatly to intensify our awareness of their thoughtlessness; the obvious way of cutting *from* the words to a reaction shot of Ratan would lessen the immediacy and our sense of the continuity of emotional development and interchange.

The whole scene is conceived in terms of a subtle interplay between separateness (editing) and contact (camera movement) that expresses the emotional flow with extraordinary precision. In the first shot, the apartness of the characters is suggested by having Ratan hovering in the background of the image while the man has his back to her. When he turns to her, Ray separates them by cutting. From there on, each time the camera moves, it is to express an inner movement toward contact. In (4), the camera tracks back to include the postmaster in the image at the moment when Ratan proudly displays her identification of the mother in the photograph and her ensuing question about the girl. Ray cuts to a close-up of Ratan; immediately she knows it is his sister, her sense of being unable to compete isolating her. In (9), the camera is at first on Ratan, then moves back to include the man; but he has his back to her and seems to have fallen asleep. The image becomes one of separation until the camera tracks in, without a cut, to show his eyes opening, the continuity of movement expressing the way the charm of the tentative, artless little song gradually gets through to him. (10) and (11) have the characters separate again as Ratan falters and admits, "That's all I know," and the postmaster laughs; but (11) continues with a track back from the close-up of him to take in Ratan as he says, "It was very good," and the two are again in emotional connection. The last shot (13), has them both in frame, with Ratan running out at the door by which she entered, reversing the movement of the opening shot of the sequence, giving the whole scene a formal symmetry. But this time the postmaster is facing her, and as she comes back and hesitates, he at last notices what she first came in to let him see, a confirmation of the new awareness of her and interest in her that has developed in the course of the scene. Hitchcock draws a distinction between "pure cinema" and "photographs of people talking,"[3] but if the concept of "pure cinema" is to have validity, it must be allowed to extend to a scene like this, in which the action is minimal and contains nothing that could not be done on a stage.

Ray's cinema is "literary" only in the sense that it is firmly rooted in narrative. He thinks primarily in terms of plot and character, and the significance of the films grow naturally out of this, extractable ideas or themes being the product rather than the starting point. In this respect, he is closer to the Hollywood masters than to European directors like Bergman, Antonioni, or Godard. Ray's own statement (the specific reference is to *Mahanagar*, but the words can be taken to apply generally) is relevant here; indeed, several of the following remarks could be taken as texts for a dissertation on Ray's work.

What I try to do in my films is to present certain situations. I try as far as possible not to comment—not to make didactic statements, not to be propagandist in any way. I merely show what it means for a family to have to change, what happens then; and certain problems are presented as clearly as possible showing all aspects, and then leave the public to draw their own conclusions. In a story like *Mahanagar*, I felt it was important to establish the fact that change was necessary, because in modern India certain ideas have to be put across. Important ideas, necessary ideas, you know. But nobody ever says in the film that you have to change or it's good to change. I merely present certain incidents, and through the incidents, and through the reaction of people to the incidents, certain facts emerge. Fairly complex facts, because there are always two sides to a thing. It's certainly not desirable that two old persons, the parents of the boy, should suffer inwardly. They suffer because they have not been able to change. But they *do* suffer and you *do* sympathize with their agony, their grief. That's how I like to present my stories, without making any kind of bombastic propaganda statements. They're stories first and foremost, they're tales, shall we say. I believe in plot; I'm not a non-believer in plot. Because India has a great tradition of stories. And it makes for a kind of orderliness which helps an audience which is not used to intellectual subtleties. And yet it affords you to be subtle in other things.

Such emphasis on plot and character, however, needs to be balanced and qualified by the "pure cinema" aspects of Ray's art, those aspects that bring the cinema closer to music than to literature. From this point of view, *Two Daughters* marks an advance on the Apu trilogy, and Ray's subsequent films show further refinements. *Charulata* tells a story, certainly, but it can also be regarded as built on a complicated pattern of echoes and cross-references, both thematic and visual, with almost every incident finding an echo somewhere, down to details of camera movement and setup. Ray himself said of this: "I'm very conscious at all times of the musical aspect of a film, of its rhythm, of its silences and of its general pattern. I'm a great lover of Mozart, and certainly I had Mozart in mind when I made *Charulata*, very much. It's consciously planned, but not worked out like a mathematical problem. I find it's more and more what emerges naturally. It's conscious and subconscious at the same time I think."

The reference to Mozart is an important clue to the nature of Ray's art. It points up his affinities with Renoir. It also helps us to connect the emphasis on the "musical" aspects of his films with the awareness that "there are always two sides to a thing"—*several* sides in a film like *Charulata* or *Days and Nights in the Forest*. The simultaneous awareness of different, even incompatible, viewpoints is a characteristic that finds supreme expression in Mozart's operas.

This emotional complexity, the delicate balancing of responses, what one might call the Mozartian aspect of Ray's art, which links him with Renoir, is already characteristic of *Pather Panchali*. It reaches fullest expression in *Days and Nights in the Forest*, the most recent of his films to reach the West at the time of writing and perhaps his masterpiece to date—certainly the most "musical" of his films. It is impossible to do it justice in a short space; a single sequence (the memory game, for example, with its extraordinary precision of nuance) would offer material for a short essay. I shall represent the film's quality by considering a single shot.

The film is about four young men from the city who go on a "back-to-nature" holiday, staying at a rest house in a forest region. Nearby, another, middle-aged, city dweller has his private holiday residence, where he is staying with his widowed daughter-in-law and his daughter, Aparna, a young lady of extreme beauty and considerable education, with whom Ashim (Soumitra Chatterjee, the adult Apu of the trilogy and one of Ray's favorite actors) begins to fall in love. The ladies drive up to the rest house when the men, stripped to the waist, are washing themselves beside a well on the grounds. General consternation and embarrassment. One man, Sanjoy, in whom the daughter-in-law has shown incipient interest, plunges to the ground behind the well; the plump, slightly clownish Sekhar, the upper part of his body covered in soap, is left to perform the necessary civilities while Ashim looks on diffidently. In a single shot, we have the car in the foreground of the image, with Aparna, in the backseat, right of screen, looking out away from the men, toward the audience, with her habitual expression of slightly enigmatic irony; Sekhar on the other side of the car, bowing and smiling ingratiatingly but writhing with embarrassment; Ashim standing in the background to the left of the image, looking toward the car, wanting contact with Aparna but feeling at a hopeless disadvantage. We are also constantly aware of Sanjoy lying prone on his belly behind the well in the far background, although we can't see him, so that he becomes an invisible but effective presence in the mise-en-scène. Ashim and Aparna are left and right of the screen, respectively, their background/foreground positioning forming an imaginary diagonal. The careful composition of the image frames Sekhar's well-intentioned, overstated bumbling between their shy silence, and Aparna's face is constantly averted from the young man in a way that underlines her awareness of him. The spectator's response is consequently divided between the comic and the tender, so that each aspect of the shot colors the others. The delicate effect of balance and counterpoint achieved here could be paralleled again and again in a film in which Ray's affinity with Mozart is even more apparent than in *Charulata*.

Except in the vague sense in which all major art is "religious" (a reaching out toward a significance beyond the individual human life lived simply for itself), Ray is not a religious director. One guesses, however, that Hinduism has its importance in the background to his work, rather as Christianity is likely to have its importance for even a nonreligious Western artist, as a generalized source and influence. But there is no temptation to devote years of scholarly research to the tracing of Hindu influences in films made perfectly intelligible by their universality of concern. A simple and convenient way of suggesting the kind of importance such an influence may have is offered by Renoir's *The River*, that harmonious union of East and West that also offers one the chance to suggest the nature of Ray's affinities with Renoir.

INTRODUCTION

When Renoir went to India to make *The River* in 1950, Ray, then working in advertising, already cherished the project of filming *Pather Panchali*, having drawn illustrations for an edition of Bannerjee's novel. He introduced himself to Renoir, for whom he already had great admiration, helped him find locations, accompanied him several times on long trips, and watched some of the shooting. He also told him the story of *Pather Panchali* ("I already had a kind of treatment in my head—it was still not written down"), and Renoir gave him enthusiastic encouragement.

The River can be regarded as Renoir's delighted discovery that he'd always been a Hindu without knowing it. From the spirit of generosity that informs *La Règle du Jeu*, with its awareness that "everyone has his reasons," to the Hindu belief that God is present in all people and all things is but a short step. Just such an awareness underlies Ray's art as well, from the ensembles of *Pather Panchali*, wherein the spectator is encouraged to experience a situation from several viewpoints simultaneously, to the Mozartian complexities of *Days and Nights in the Forest*. The single shot I described from the latter film is sufficient in itself to suggest the spirit that links Ray's art to Renoir's.

Even more interesting in relation to Ray's work—and to the trilogy, perhaps most of all—are the references in *The River* to the goddess Kali and their connection with the film's central image, the giant peepul tree. Kali is the goddess of destruction and creation, "for without destruction there can be no creation." She could perhaps be regarded as the presiding deity of the Apu films, with their recurrent motif of simultaneous loss and gain. The central unifying thematic preoccupation of all Ray's work to date is change or "progress": again and again he returns to an investigation of people's attitudes to change, how they cope with it (or fail to cope), the gaps it produces between generations or between people from cultural backgrounds at different stages of development. And the overall attitude to "progress" is consistently ambivalent: what is created is always balanced (though not negated) by what is destroyed. The peepul tree in *The River* is sacred to women, who bring to it offerings in the hope of being fertile and producing male children: within its recesses lives a cobra, which kills the only son of the British family who are the film's central characters. The flowing of the river itself is used by Renoir to suggest the continuity of life; the character relationships in the film continually hint at a balancing of gain and loss, the death of the child bringing a new understanding and closeness to the people near him, the end of innocence being the start of maturity. Such concerns, and the attitude to life they imply, are by no means restricted in Renoir's work to *The River*, but it is only in that film that their affinities with Hinduism become manifest. Perhaps it was Hinduism that attracted Renoir to India and attracted Satyajit Ray to Renoir.

Although a considerable time gap and two other films intervened between the shooting of *Aparajito* and the shooting of *The World of Apu*, although Apu himself is incarnated by three different actors in the course of the trilogy, and although each film makes sense if seen in isolation, it is nevertheless possible to trace a clear structure in the trilogy as a whole and to view it as one long film in three parts.

Apu is the only character who appears in all three films, and (obviously enough) it is his development that provides the trilogy with its main unifying impulse. One striking overall structural feature is the way in which the focus is progressively narrowed, so that our attention is concentrated more and more exclusively on Apu himself. Although in an important sense he is already central to *Pather Panchali*, it is essentially an ensemble film, our interest being involved in the complex interplay between the five members of the family rather than directed exclusively toward any one of them. *Aparajito* begins as a trio (Apu and his parents) and dwindles to a duet (Apu and his mother). *The World of Apu*, despite its title, is more about Apu than his world, and his developing consciousness is more unequivocally central to the film than to its forerunners. This is true even in the sequences depicting Apu's marriage, as can be seen by comparing these with Ray's handling of the mother-son relationship in *Aparajito*. The overall effect that most decisively characterizes the earlier film is achieved by the division of our consciousness, hence of our sympathetic allegiance, between mother and son; we see Sarbojaya more fully than Apu ever quite does and share her emotions in ways he can't allow himself to. Our awareness of Aparna, on the other hand, is scarcely separable from Apu's. Only in the closing stretches of *The World of Apu* is the central position of Apu's consciousness challenged: the end of the trilogy is really a new beginning, and this is expressed structurally in the way in which the consciousness of Apu's son is allowed equality (in the presentation of the action) with Apu's own.

This progressive concentration of focus on the trilogy's protagonist is accompanied by the removal through death of the people nearest him. There are no less than five important deaths in the trilogy: Auntie, the aged female dependent, and

Sarbojaya after Apu leaves for the city in *Aparajito*.

Apu's sister, Durga, in *Pather Panchali*; Apu's parents in *Aparajito*; Apu's wife, Aparna, in *The World of Apu*. Of these, three seem to have a special structural significance: those of the three females who have a decisive influence on Apu's life: sister, mother, wife. They are roughly equidistant in the trilogy: Durga's death occurs near the end of the first film, Sarbojaya's at the end of the second, Aparna's approximately midway through the third. Each, at the time of her death, is the person emotionally closest to Apu. One special recurring circumstance in the three deaths heightens our sense of them as a leitmotiv running through the trilogy: each death takes place at a time of separation. It is true that we share intimately in the mother's experience of Durga's death, but

INTRODUCTION

the irrevocable fact of it is brought home most forcefully when Ray leads us sympathetically to share the father's shock when, returning home, he learns what has happened. Sarbojaya dies alone before Apu can get home to her. Aparna dies in childbirth several days' journey away from her husband. In each case, the fact of absence greatly intensifies the sense of loss, of human helplessness in the face of death's abruptness and finality, and of life's terrible unpredictability.

But the deaths, felt as so terrible in themselves, are never merely negative in results. Throughout the trilogy, loss is usually accompanied by gain, and each death leads, either immediately or indirectly, to progress. Durga's death provides the family's final incentive to leave the village for the city; Sarbojaya's releases Apu to follow his own path untrammeled; Aparna's, the most painful of all, leads him eventually (the effect is far more delayed) to a complete maturity and fully adult depth, out of which grows his ability to accept the child with joy. Our dual sense of Apu's emotional rebirth and the boy's release into a new and fuller life with the father whose lack has so disturbed his early childhood provides the whole trilogy with its emotional climax and culmination. The boy is very like the young Apu. Life has come full circle, but it has also advanced: the life into which Apu will be able to initiate his son is richer in potentialities for development than that into which Apu himself was born. It is not just a matter of physical environment, the city opposed to the village: the crucial presence in the child's environment will be Apu himself, with his hard-won maturity and affirmation.

The trilogy certainly encourages one to draw the inference that the progress from the primitive village of *Pather Panchali*

In *Pather Panchali*, Apu looks at the train, another unifying leitmotif.

to the city of *The World of Apu* constitutes an advance; but the point mustn't be allowed to stand unqualified. Ray is by no means a simpleminded believer in progress, and the sense of advance at the end of the trilogy will be modified for us, if we glance back over all that has led up to it, by, again, a sense of corresponding loss. If the life Apu has won through to is incomparably richer in potentialities than that into which he was born, it is also fraught with far greater problems and uncertainties. The obvious comparison is with *The Rainbow* (though it must be conceded at once that the trilogy suffers somewhat beside the extraordinary range and density of Lawrence's great novel): Apu's progress through the trilogy to some extent corresponds to the movement from the comparative stability of the Marsh farm, with its rootedness in a defined cultural tradition, its known and tested values, to the bewildering contemporary complexities (and they *still* feel contemporary, almost sixty years after the book was written) that Ursula Brangwen faces in the latter part of the book. The possibilities life offers in the village of *Pather Panchali* are too meager for the comparison to be very close—Lawrence's characters are never forced by necessity to squander their emotional and physical energies on the bare basic business of sustaining life—but the movement of the trilogy from a united (if poverty-stricken) family within a clearly defined (if extremely limited) community to an isolated individual in a great city is, as in *The Rainbow*, a movement of social history as much as a narrative about individual characters.

The ambivalence of the trilogy's attitude to "progress" is epitomized rather beautifully in the development of its most obvious unifying motif: the train. There is nothing forced or arbitrary about Ray's use of train images as a unifying device. There is no simple symbolism involved. The meaning of the images shifts and changes and accumulates complex emotional overtones as the trilogy progresses. From the magical moment in *Pather Panchali* when the sound of a distant train first impinges on the child Apu's consciousness as the family sit in their home at night, to the adult Apu's attempted suicide on the railway tracks amid the squalor of a Calcutta slum in *The World of Apu*, is a movement that should remove any suspicion that the concept of "progress" in the trilogy—and in Ray's work generally—is simple or naïve.

PATHER PANCHALI

Apu is born near the beginning of *Pather Panchali*, and we see him briefly as a baby, being sung to by the senile female dependent known as "Auntie." However, our real introduction to him comes when, some years having elapsed, we see him being awakened by Durga in time for school. The way in which he is presented is critical to his role in *Pather Panchali* and to some extent in the whole trilogy. The sequence of shots is as follows: (1) Durga enters the yard, followed by a cat. The camera pans left with her, to take in Auntie shaking her bed rag to air it. The mother, Sarbojaya, crosses the image on her way to fetch water. At the end of the shot, only Auntie and the cat are left in the frame. (2) Durga shakes Apu, who is completely concealed under a tattered blanket. (3) A closer shot: Durga pries open a hole in the covering with her fingers. (4) A larger close-up shows Apu's closed eye within the hole. The eye suddenly opens and looks out. (5) Durga shakes him again. (6) Apu sits up. Rapid dissolve to (7) Apu cleaning his teeth, which introduces a series of shots linked by dissolves showing Durga combing Apu's hair, Apu

Sarbojaya, Durga, and Apu

drinking milk and having his face wiped, and the children moving along the path to school, toward a cloudy horizon beyond the flat fields.

The first shot, apparently very simple and containing no "significant" action, is characteristic of the style and method of *Pather Panchali* in several ways. The characters are in long shot throughout, so that we are aware of them within their environment and in relation to each other. The women of three generations are shown going about their ordinary daily routines, each separate, scarcely aware of each other, yet linked by the continuity of the take. The effect here, as of many comparable "group" shots in the film, is of different lives being lived simultaneously, at once separate and interconnected. Cutting from one to the other—the "documentary" way of clarifying and emphasizing their various chores—would have destroyed the sense of family and the sense of life continuing in time, the items in a montage tending to appear fixed and timeless. With Ray, one is repeatedly aware of flux within the image.

The age-death-continuity motif, important throughout the trilogy but central to *Pather Panchali*, is unobtrusively present not only in the linking of three generations within a single take. In the sequence leading up to Apu's birth, Auntie is visually linked in several shots with white kittens. For example: Durga is sent to return the fruit she has stolen from the local landowner's orchard. In one shot, we see Durga run out of the frame at the left, Auntie in the foreground rinsing her mouth (she has been eating the fruit Durga stole), and the kittens entering the frame from the right. When Auntie, threatened with expulsion by Sarbojaya, indignantly packs her bundle to leave, she hurls it out onto a kitten playing in the dust. Durga follows Auntie to try to bring her back, Sarbojaya calls her in to sweep the yard, and we see the three kittens playing as she sets to work. The association of the senile and useless Auntie with the "new life" of the kittens is referred to again in the shot we are considering; only now the cat is full grown, and there is only one. The *waste* of life in the natural world is almost subliminally suggested; and in Auntie herself, we see what life, in the environment depicted, can become. The figure is presented quite unsentimentally: we are led to see her as selfish and grotesque. But this never detracts from the pathos of her situation, useless and generally unwanted, with no aim or purpose beyond cadging bits of food.

The first shot of the sequence, then, serves to provide the context into which Apu is introduced: a metaphysical context (however sketchy at this point) as much as a physical one, for Ray's method itself, with its emphasis on continuity and flux, implies a metaphysic, and he is offering us something more than a documentary study of poverty in a primitive community. The key image is the eye that opens and looks out. Apu in *Pather Panchali* is not so much a character as a developing consciousness. Our relationship with him is a complex one. We are never invited simply to identify with him, and Ray's customary objectivity of presentation applies to Apu as to the other characters. He is consistently a part of the *ensemble*. At the same time, in scene after scene we are brought back to an awareness of him as a registering consciousness. We are led to see the action with a double vision: we see partly through Apu's eyes, partly through our own adult consciousness. Instead of simply identifying us with the child's view, Ray makes us increasingly sensitive to the child's *reactions* to what he sees, his storing up of experiences and perceptions, his part-intuitive, part-contemplative way of reaching the decisions that help determine his own nature, the formation of his own outlook on the world in which he lives and grows. Immediately after the sequence I have described comes the scene of Apu at the village school. The schoolmaster is also the shopkeeper—not at fixed separate hours but simultaneously. The "lesson" consists of the teacher mouthing out a poem and shouting at his pupils as he weighs food and chats with customers. He yawns undisguisedly; Apu and a classmate play tic-tac-toe; an old man comes in for a gossip. When Apu grins at them, the teacher bellows, "What's so funny? Is this a comedy?" and grabs a cane—with which he then

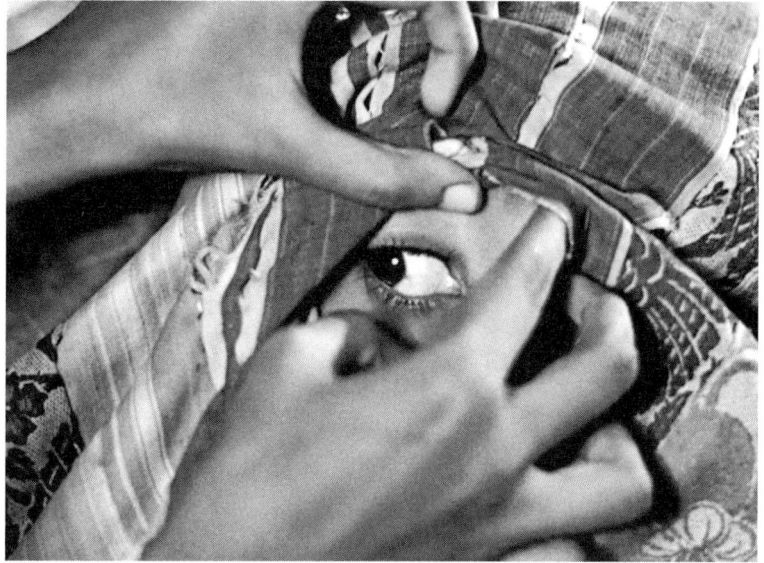

The gazing eye of Apu.

scratches his back, either too indolent or too unsure of his ground to use it for chastisement. The scene is very funny, but its prime function is a serious one: the demonstration that if Apu, the alert open eye, is going to learn and develop, it will not be at school. There are four extended sequences in the film where we see Apu undergoing formative experiences and reaching decisions about life—the quarrel over the stolen necklace, the children's first view of a train, the death of Durga, the preparations for departure—and I want to examine each of these in detail.

The sequence of the quarrel over the stolen necklace offers beautiful examples of Ray's subtlety and inexplicitness, his method of presenting an action with great analytical clarity while leaving the audience free to ponder a significance he

Durga gives Auntie the stolen fruit.

refuses to underline by means of close-ups or emphatic acting: the significant details are there as parts of a whole situation, the integrity of which Ray is careful to preserve. Underlying this may be the characteristic Hindu sense that (in the words of Professor Godbole in *A Passage to India*) "nothing can be performed in isolation." In any case, Ray is one of the cinema's great masters of interrelatedness.

The sequence begins with a close-up of a dog in which we see Apu pointing an arrow fixed in a rudimentary homemade bow. Sarbojaya calls Apu for his food and feeds him with her fingers. But Apu soon runs off to play, and the food is given to the dog. By the simplest means, the shots suggest Apu's eagerness for experience and activity—his impatience with such

The schoolmaster.

commonplace occupations as eating—and his resourcefulness in inventing means to satisfy such urges within the limitations of his environment: we never see him bored.

The wealthy land-owning neighbor appears, to accuse Durga of stealing her daughter's necklace. Durga apparently isn't present, but the box in which she keeps her accumulation of trivial but treasured possessions is produced and its contents brutally strewn on the ground. Then Sarbojaya sees Apu furtively gesturing Durga away and calls the girl out from behind the crumbling wall where she is hiding. We already sense a conflict of feelings within the woman: on the one hand, her desire to be socially respected for honesty and to avoid any accusation that she fails to bring up her children properly; on the other, her protective maternal feelings for the girl. Durga has just returned from stealing fruit in the neighbor's orchard. Sarbojaya defends her, saying she might steal fruit but wouldn't take anything valuable. The neighbor leaves, complaining loudly to another villager, "Like mother, like daughter." Ray's staging of the scene beautifully expresses and keeps in balance the family tensions and loyalties. The father, Hari, isn't present, but all the other members of the family either implicitly or explicitly involve themselves in Durga's delinquency. The mother defends her verbally (in a way that half condones fruit stealing), Apu expresses his instinctive complicity by gesturing her away, and although Auntie, present throughout the scene, is as usual not going to commit herself, we know that the fruit was stolen partly for her. It is worth stressing at this point—casting a glance ahead to the ending of the film— that our sympathy for Durga does not depend on any assumption that she is being unjustly accused. We are, I think, uncertain about this, but it is psychologically plausible that she is guilty. Growing up in poverty, she is deprived of most of the material pleasures of life, and the neighbor makes her particularly aware of this, unkindly emphasizing her own children's better fortune. Even more important, because more universal in its significance, is the implication that even within Durga's own family it is Apu who is the favored child. The tendency to favor the male child over the female, especially strong in primitive cultures in which the possible destiny of a Durga is to end up an "Auntie," is to some extent common to all. Sarbojaya unhesitatingly takes the boy's side in quarrels, and when the children want money for anything, Durga sends Apu to plead for it, although she is the elder. Her little hoard of possessions becomes the more pathetic when one sees it as an attempt to compensate for a permanent and continually aggravated sense of disadvantage.

We are made to feel acutely the humiliation of mother and daughter: Durga's not so much at the accusation as at the way her treasures, precious to her, are treated with thoughtless contempt by the adults, emptied out of the box like rubbish onto the dusty earth, and then ignored; Sarbojaya's above all at the other woman's closing remarks, insolently spoken to be overheard, as if they summed up the judgment of the whole community. It is the mother's humiliation that precipitates the rest of the action in the sequence. In a fury of frustration, she pulls Durga by the hair, watched by both Auntie and Apu, drags her to the gate (leaving a trail of stolen berries), and throws her out. There is

Durga watches the quarrel about the necklace.

Auntie.

a painful sense that she is acting against her own most deeply human instincts, that she is punishing Durga not for the proven theft of fruit or even for the unproven theft of the necklace but for her own humiliation—social pressures (the public accusation that she is not bringing up her children properly) overpowering her maternal sympathies. Apu's evident shock at his mother's behavior is partly shared by the spectator, though qualified by our adult insight into emotions beyond the child's comprehension. Durga's punishment culminates in a climactic shot whose visual balance offers a particularly fine example of the complexity of response that Ray's objectivity can provoke. The center of the screen is occupied by the broken wall. Outside the wall, left of screen, Durga limps off, weeping; behind the gate, right of screen,

Sarbojaya collapses, also weeping. The spectator's sympathy is divided precisely as the image is divided.

We then see Auntie picking up Durga's treasures and putting them back in the box: even Auntie, usually preoccupied with her own meager comforts, has been shocked by the emotional rawness of the scene into performing a tenderly considerate action. We have so far been aware of Apu more as a witness, a receptive consciousness, than a participant. There is now another of Ray's characteristic "group" shots in which Apu crosses the yard, passes his weeping mother, passes Auntie, and rinses out his mouth with water. The action seems merely casual and irrelevant until we reflect back on the opening of the scene, in which Sarbojaya fed him with her fingers: he is now—albeit unconsciously— expressing his repudiation of her decisions and her influence. The long-shot, single-take continuity prevents any laboring of the point, which is just naturally and unobtrusively *there*, an integral part of the action; it also counterbalances our response to what amounts to a moral judgment on Apu's part by keeping us aware of the mother's continuing grief and shame (now clearly shame at her own actions) and the old woman's more passive, less accusatory expression of sympathy for Durga. With the mother still weeping by the gate, Apu then reads arithmetic problems (about buying apples!) out loud. In retrospect from *Aparajito*, it strikes one as something of a key moment in his development: book learning in the family is exclusively associated with Hari, the father, Sarbojaya remaining completely uneducated. Apu is turning—and not without ostentation—from his mother's to his father's influence and to the education that will increasingly separate him from Sarbojaya. The scene is an admirable example of

Sarbojaya works, Hari meditates.

Ray's ability to express his character's unconscious psychological impulses through actions.

The train is a recurrent image throughout the trilogy. On its first appearance, in the scene that immediately precedes the stolen necklace incident—when it is not even an image, merely a sound in the night—it is juxtaposed with Apu's education: his father is teaching him to write. The children hear the train, and Apu asks where it is. "Let's go someday," he says, and Hari praises his work. The train suggests, obviously, a means of movement to a wider world where educational possibilities are less restricted; but its primary association here is with progress itself. The scene has two other main components: Sarbojaya is doing Durga's hair, and the girl, on the threshold of puberty, is trying to thread a needle, with extreme short-sighted concentration and little success. The sound of the train suddenly puts all the scene's components in a new perspective, evoking a world of knowledge and achievement that "places" the old woman's primitivism and holds out possibilities for the children's development that are beyond their imagination.

The scene in which Durga and Apu see a train for the first time is—justifiably—the most famous in the film. But it is impossible, here again, to consider the train imagery in isolation. Its meaning (or more accurately, perhaps, its emotional force) is determined by a context of interacting developments. It is necessary to go back at least to the play performed by a traveling company that Apu watches in the village. The scene is a good example of the double vision Ray encourages in the spectator in *Pather Panchali*: we see the play with our own eyes as an absurd melodrama, clumsily staged, with crude ranting actors (one made up as a girl to play the heroine); we also see it through Apu's eyes and sympathetically experience his wonder at a new world of imagination and passion opening out before him. The play is in a different language from that spoken in the film (the distributors are clearly right not to subtitle it), and the entire text is presumably meaningless to Apu; but he is thrilled by the spectacle, the magic of dressing up and pretending, of imitating heroic lives and passions remote from the realm of immediate experience.

The quarrel between Durga and Apu that leads to their first sight of the train is precipitated by Apu's imaginative reaction to the play. We see him putting on a homemade moustache and crown, cut from silver foil, which Durga recognizes as taken

Apu dresses up.

from her box of treasures. She chases Apu, catches him, beats him, and is rebuked by their mother. So Durga, impotent and frustrated, runs off, with rude, angry gestures. Apu follows; we see them running across the open fields beyond the trees that surround the village; the camera tilts up to show the sky, the open country, anticipating the emotional release that will follow the present tensions.

The remainder of the sequence is built by intercutting the children's experience of the train and the death of Auntie, until the two actions are united as the children return and find her dying. Earlier, before the play scene, we saw Auntie turned out by Sarbojaya, not for the first time: the old woman had wheedled a neighbor into buying her the shawl that Hari couldn't afford, and Sarbojaya took this (following shortly after the stolen necklace incident) as a further humiliation. Then, immediately before the scene of the play, there came a brief but eloquent moment showing the children playing, running past a pond beside which Auntie stood motionless. The rejection of sentimentality in the presentation of Auntie is maintained right through to her death: we are never invited to respond on the Sweet Old Lady level or nudged into feeling for her anything beyond the compassion her situation naturally provokes. She is an infuriating, selfish, useless old human being. The uselessness of her life, to herself as much as to others, is made abundantly clear: she lives only for the next bit of stolen fruit or a new shawl. She and Durga are fond of each other; there is a fragile bond between them (which the old woman exploits), based perhaps on their shared sense of being superfluous. Otherwise, Auntie has outlived all real connection with anyone. On the other hand, no one could accuse Ray of callousness or suppose him to be preaching geronticide. Auntie clutches tenaciously at life and enjoys the meager benefits presented to her. The shot of her standing in hopeless immobility by the pond as the children run past brings home to us the importance, to such a life, of the family, however tenuous her vital connection with its individual members. Suddenly, removed from them, she has literally nothing to do, not even a plant to sprinkle water on: there is no point in going forward or going back, no point even in sitting down: it is an image of the most ultimate isolation.

After we watch Durga and Apu run off across the fields, Ray returns us to the yard of their home. Auntie hobbles back in, saying, "I'm not feeling well." The seriousness of her condition is clear at once, not only from her appearance but from the difference between this humble plea for compassion and the stubborn pride she showed earlier, at the time of Apu's birth, when she refused to return until Durga gave her the pretext of seeing her new "nephew." But Sarbojaya tells her brutally that this is not her home: we sense that she is almost deliberately suppressing her awareness of the old woman's need. From the enclosed yard and the helpless, dying old woman, Ray cuts to a shot of Durga chewing cane, taken from a low angle so that we see only the sky as background; Apu edges into the frame in long shot, wanting to make peace, wanting not to be excluded. The enclosure/openness antithesis unobtrusively reinforces the age/youth opposition.

Back to Auntie. She asks for water and is told, "Get it yourself," although the water pot is near Sarbojaya. Again one senses that the younger woman is deliberately hardening her heart: there is not enough food for the children, and a dependent old woman is expendable. Auntie's forehead is beaded with sweat as she struggles to the water; Sarbojaya, with a sudden involuntary concession to humanity, raises the lid of the pot for her. A close-up: Auntie turns on Sarbojaya a toothless, ingratiating smile, which fades pathetically as she sees it has failed to ingratiate. She drinks, then sprinkles her head with water; Sarbojaya is preparing food that Auntie will not be invited to share, licking her fingers, trying to ignore the old woman. Auntie sprinkles the last drops of water on the plant we saw her watering early in the film, collects her bundle, and hobbles out of the yard: it is as if she has silently accepted her doom, accepted that she has no right to protest or plead. Now that Auntie's back is turned, Sarbojaya watches her. As she disappears from view, the dog at which Apu tried to shoot the arrow is in the foreground of the image. Ray repeatedly associates the old woman with the animal world (kittens, dog), where death is casual, almost unnoticed. Her last attention to the plant is a beautiful touch, so "right" psychologically—the desire to leave something of herself behind in the world that is discarding her—that any symbolic meaning one feels it to have is inseparable from its direct significance in the action.

Throughout the scene, Ray retains our sympathy for Sarbojaya without ever minimizing the brutality of what she is doing. We are led to understand so well her *need* to be brutal: if she let herself feel anything, the family, struggling against starvation already, would be burdened with a completely helpless invalid. The one small humanizing detail, when she involuntarily raises the lid of the water pot that she has refused to carry to the old woman, eloquently expresses the instincts for kindness that she is fighting down.

From the shot of the dog and Auntie's departure, Ray cuts to a shot of electric wires, with a whirring, humming noise on the soundtrack. We see Durga with the cane in her mouth, still, listening. Apu approaches, still wearing his silver-foil crown, the presence of which throughout the scene keeps in our minds not only the children's quarrel but the play, thereby linking Apu's two "educational" experiences. Cattle are grazing in the background; feathery seeded grasses grow in the field by the pylon. Apu puts his head against the pylon and listens; Durga wanders among the grasses, vaguely troubled by what she doesn't understand. The cut from Auntie to the wires seems at first to make a simple opposition of primitivism and progress; but the ensuing images complicate this by juxtaposing the machine-made hardness of the wires and pylon with the sensuous and pliant beauty of the seeded grasses. Apu, fascinated, wanders through a magically beautiful world of grasses taller than he is; again the spectator becomes conscious of a dual vision, sympathetically responding with Apu to the novel wonder of the pylon and simultaneously feeling the natural beauty that the pylon disfigures.

Durga throws the cane to Apu: we sense that her uneasiness at the novelty makes her need the reassurance of human contact. Apu grins, seeing that he is forgiven and that contact is to be resumed. Durga tells him to chew on the cane; their uneasiness at the new experience of the machinery imperceptibly reconciles them. He asks what the pylon is. Durga can't answer but tells him to listen. They stand up, looking around. With the children in the foreground of the image, we see a trail of black smoke rising, moving above the white, sensuous grasses. Then there is a shot of the train crossing the horizon, near the top of the frame, as Durga and Apu run toward it, vanishing from sight into the grasses. From a shot of Apu running toward the embankment, Ray cuts to a shot from the other side of the tracks. We momentarily see Apu running before he disappears from view, the embankment intervening; then the train passes, blackening the whole image, and we glimpse Apu again in long shot between the wheels. Ray's decision to present the child's experience in this way, and to distance us from it, is crucial. The obvious thing would have been to present it subjectively: close-up of Apu's face, close-up of train, then back to the child, expressing his wonder. Ray puts us on the other side of the tracks, to look at Apu's experience

Apu, Durga, and the train.

rather than simply to share it. Hence, we bring to it our own adult experience of "progress" and technology and cities: the train obliterates the landscape and shatters its serenity; Apu becomes a tiny, frail figure dwarfed to insignificance. The sequence is crowned by a carefully composed landscape shot that unites the scene's chief components: the grasses filling the bottom of the screen, the top blackened by smoke, the image framed between telegraph poles on the left, a signal on the right.

In long shot, we see Durga and Apu returning home, laughing and chattering, completely reunited, carrying a water pot and leading a calf: the precise continuity from the previous scene isn't clear, but the children's mood establishes an *emotional* continuity. Without a cut, the camera moves to the right to reveal

Auntie sitting among the bamboos; the laughter of the children continues on the soundtrack. The following series of shots show Apu leading the calf; Durga creeping up on Auntie, then shaking her; Apu grinning. Then Auntie suddenly rolls over. The children run home; the water pot is dropped in a stream. In long shot, we see the calf running, pulling Apu; then the camera pans down to show Auntie—again the two are linked within a single shot, a life ending, a life developing. The old woman is still breathing feebly, but it is clear that she will never regain consciousness.

Auntie dies, Apu sees a train: a moment of decisive transition from the primitive world of the past to an advanced world of the future. That is, certainly, the dominant idea of the sequence; but it is modified and rendered complex by other factors. Against the "negative" of the useless old woman's meaningless death, the train is not the only positive. There is also the life in nature, the calf, the stream, the seeded grass, the play of sunlight and shadow among the trees: a serene, harmonious world that the train temporarily blotted out. And there is the emphasis on family feeling: the resolution of the children's quarrel and their quite unselfconscious affection for and dependence on each other; our sense that what little "meaning" Auntie's life had was conferred on it by her acceptance within the family group. The sequence is very far from being a simpleminded statement about progress: Ray's films don't make "statements" of that sort. Rather, what we have is a complex texture in which various emotional strands interweave. If the *overall* movement of Ray's first film is from the primitive to a yearned-for "progress," we may also recall that one of his most recent films (*Days and Nights in the Forest*) is about four young men from the city who

Durga with the calf.

The death of Auntie.

return briefly to a primitive community to seek—and partly find—solace and renewal.

Durga's death is the first example in the trilogy of the death-in-separation motif: Hari is far away in the city, trying to make money as a professional prayer caller, to support the family. As usual, the incident must be felt in its context to be fully appreciated. Two threads in particular lead up to it, contributing to its emotional effect: the suggestions of the family's increasing poverty, with the sense that they are actually nearing starvation level, and the wedding of Durga's friend. Sarbojaya sells the family's possessions to buy rice; no word comes from Hari for months. Durga (who had earlier expressed a foreboding that she would never get married) attends the wedding, staring at the bride with mingled envy and affection. A neighbor rebukes Sarbojaya for keeping secret the family's plight. At last a postcard comes from Hari: his affairs have improved; he will be back soon with money.

Ray dissolves from the scene of the postcard to a short sequence showing water flies on a pond, accompanied by a joyful outburst of Ravi Shankar music. The initial effect is of a kind of celebration: the father is returning, the family's troubles are over, nature is alive and fertile, a harmonious world of water plants, insects, blossoms. But another traditional association of blossoms and water flies is with transience: the sequence is immediately followed by that in which Durga catches pneumonia. The dual associations make of the water-fly passage a perfect transition, the effect of which is completed by passing from the insects to domestic animals. The sequence of the coming of the monsoon begins with the now familiar dog and kitten, idle in the heat. But the kitten, though indistinguishable from its predecessors, is, of course, of another generation. Life renews itself perpetually and in profusion, but, with our developed human sense of individuality, this is only half a consolation.

The camera moves down from a caged bird to show Sarbojaya fanning herself. Durga, meanwhile, is making up her eyes, applying the traditional spot at the top of her nose, between the eyebrows. She is of marriageable age, her imagination bent on following the example of her friend. Accompanying this image are the sounds of thunder. Then we see Apu outside, against a background of stormy skies. Durga performs a curious little ritual with a plant, which presumably means something specific for Indian audiences but which in terms of recurrent imagery links clearly enough with Auntie's watering of a plant (twice) earlier: apparently another "renewal," or continuity, image. Durga then runs out after Apu.

There follow further intimations of the imminence of the monsoon: lily leaves on the pond curl over in the wind; Sarbojaya calls Durga and begins to get the washing in. We see an old man sitting by the pond, hunched up, asleep; a drop of rain falls on his bald head. Then comes the downpour: Apu runs under a big tree; the dog runs into the house. Durga, already soaked, delightedly washes her face in the pouring rain, sticking out her tongue at her brother as he shelters under his tree nearby. They huddle together under the tree; she covers him with her shawl. She chants a rhyme to stop the rain, then suddenly sneezes. Ray dissolves to the doctor's visit: Durga is in bed, very ill. Apu asks her, "Shall we go see the trains again?"

Then it is night. Durga is worse. Another, more violent storm begins. Sarbojaya applies cloths to Durga's forehead, and against this helpless, inadequate act of tenderness, Ray sets details implying the fury of the storm: the rag of curtain blows in the gusts; the wick burning in the oil flickers; the door moves inward from its frame as the wind strikes it; a shelf on which a small idol sits in imperturbable contemplation stirs. There is a flash of lightning; the tattered curtain blows down; the door bursts open. If one is tempted to describe the Ray of *Pather Panchali* as a "nature poet," in the sense in which Wordsworth was a nature poet—an artist, that is to say, centrally concerned with man-in-nature, not with mere decorative description—one has to add that he is never guilty of the kind of sentimental simplifications ("Knowing that Nature never did betray / The heart that loved her")[4] to which Wordsworth was prone. From the idyllic, "lyrical" sequence of the water flies and water blossoms, we have passed very swiftly to something very like the world of Hitchcock's *The Birds*: a world where nothing is certain, where terrible destructive forces can be unleashed without warning. For Indian audiences, the coming of the monsoon itself carries implications of the renewal of life, giving Durga's death an inherent irony: the life-giving rain in which she ecstatically bathed her face and hair is also the rain that kills her. The image of the idol sitting on the shelf is a marvelously economical comment on the precariousness of human comforts, of belief in a benevolently guided universe.

Apu is sent to fetch a friend of his mother. He passes the ruined yard: we see a litter of overturned and broken pots, damaged fencing, a dead frog, the calf standing in its roofless, flooded pen, a cooking pot hanging uselessly. Durga is dead; the friend tries to comfort Sarbojaya. Then we see Apu by the pond, cleaning his teeth with his finger. His hand suddenly becomes

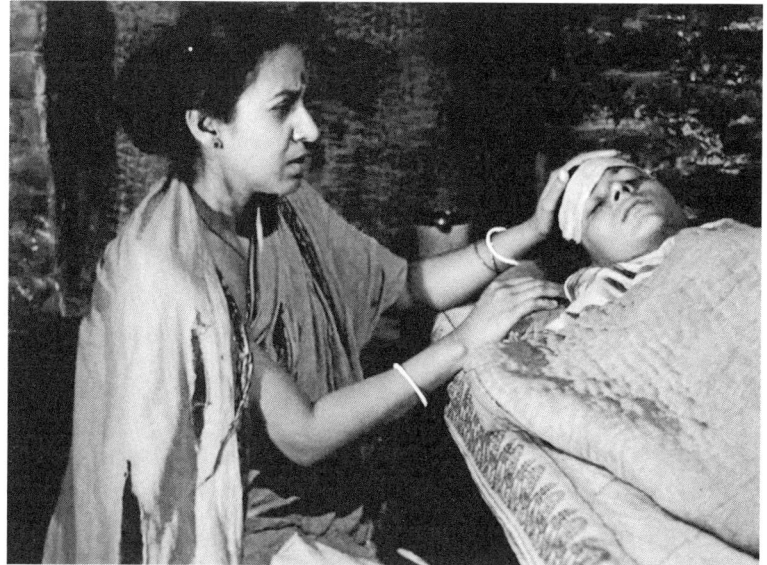

Sarbojaya nurses Durga.

still, suspended. Sarbojaya draws water, Apu does his own hair, daily routine is resumed, and life goes on. But these actions recapitulate things we saw Durga doing earlier: particularly, they recall our introduction to the child Apu, when Durga awakened him for school. Now Apu leaves for school alone, carrying an umbrella: the detail, visually slightly comic, becomes touchingly so in its context of Durga's death from pneumonia.

At this point, Hari returns. He calls Apu, finds the wrecked yard, the cow and calf without shelter. He calls Durga. His wife comes out to him, seeming numb, incapable of response. He proudly opens the presents he has brought, to conceal his disquiet from himself, culminating in Durga's new sari: "Our worries are over." The camera moves up to show Sarbojaya's face streaming

Hari, returning home with presents, learns of Durga's death.

with tears, as the music on the soundtrack laments wildly for her. There follows a shot beautifully controlled in its intensity. Sarbojaya collapses. The camera moves up and tracks in to Hari's face as he realizes what has happened. He half rises: his head moves out of frame, and the camera remains on his bent knees and poised hands, the most intense emotion—the sense of a brief moment of agonizing duration—conveyed by the physical suspension and the way it is framed. Then he too sinks down. The camera tracks back as Hari cries out agonizedly for the child he will never see again. Then there is a cut to Apu on his way to school, the absurd umbrella under his arm, arrested by the pond, listening to his father's cries.

The construction of this whole sequence, it will now be evident, takes up the pattern already established in the film.

Throughout it, Apu is not particularly singled out as a center of attention: Durga, Sarbojaya, and Hari have at least equal prominence, the mother's anxiety and grief and the father's shock being the dominant emotions. But Ray returns us to Apu at the end, and the experiences depicted take on their final significance as registered within *his* experience. Precisely what effect Durga's death has on him Ray doesn't tell us: *could* the experience of his sister's death, his mother's despair, the discovery of the precariousness of life and the essential indifference of nature, be conveyed in a simple statement? The two moments of reflection—when his finger pauses as he cleans his teeth and when he hears his father's cries—say nothing and say everything: Ray doesn't simplify or schematize.

In a sense, the real climax of *Pather Panchali*, the point to which the film builds, is not Durga's death but its aftermath—or, more precisely, one apparently tiny incident that the death indirectly provokes. Hari decides to take what is left of his family to the city. We see him sorting his books and papers. Then, as the elders of the village arrive for leave-taking, he sends Apu to bring some things from a high, seldom-used shelf. As Hari talks of going to Benares, Apu runs in and out in front of the old men, in the foreground of the image: he plays no part in the conversation, but it is *his* future that Ray keeps in our minds. Then there is a shot from behind the shelf as Apu reaches up to pull down a dusty, cobweb-covered bowl. The voices continue on the soundtrack: "Won't you ever return here?" "Perhaps Apu will when he grows up." In the bowl (from which a spider hastily scuttles), half hidden by the thick cobwebs, is the stolen necklace; Durga was guilty after all. The counterpointing of image and dialogue is important: this is indeed a place to which one feels Apu will return, in memory, when he grows up. He takes the necklace, flings it in the pond, and remains watching, motionless, until the water weeds have completely re-covered the spot.

Throughout the film, we have been returned, repeatedly, to Apu experiencing, learning, absorbing, developing. Here, for the first time in the trilogy, we see him confronted with the necessity for making a conscious moral decision, though "conscious" is to some extent misleading—one isn't led to suppose that Apu could *explain* his actions. I'm not sure that the critic should try to explain them either: to explain is often, in effect, to simplify. Apu's decision is motivated by more than a simple desire to preserve his sister's memory unblemished. In the row about the necklace, he

The village elders come for Hari's leave-taking.

sided with Durga implicitly: emotionally, he is involved as an accomplice. More intangibly, his feelings about both his mother and his father play a not precisely definable part: on the one hand, his memory of his mother's humiliation and the revenge she took on Durga for having caused it; on the other, his identification with his impractical, dreamy, idealistic father who obeys his own emotional drifts rather than external moral dictates. Sarbojaya called Durga out from hiding to be publicly humiliated, putting social feelings (her desire to appear righteous and honest) before personal (maternal tenderness); in finally removing the evidence, Apu is confirming his repudiation of his mother's values. One might be tempted, more simply, to say that the primary motive is the child's natural impulse to put from him and bury moral and emotional problems he can't yet adequately cope with, as the boy Johan in Bergman's *The Silence* hides the old waiter's funeral photographs under the carpet (hides them, essentially, from *himself*). But no sooner has one made the comparison than important differences spring to mind: the associations of the necklace are much more present and personal to Apu than those of the photographs to Johan and are consequently felt as closer to conscious formulation; and the more conscious the associations, the less explainable the actions in terms of blind instinct.

All this said, I am scarcely more confident that the motivation behind the concealment of the necklace has been adequately accounted for, and this seems to me a strength in the film rather than a weakness. Ray isn't cheating by evading difficulties or glossing over them; he is respecting the essential mystery and integrity of the individual psyche. The effect is of psychological density, not thinness. The whole of Apu's life is felt to be behind his actions at this point, and the underlying assumption is that a whole life, not merely a single motive, is behind *every* decision. We come upon this assumption again and again in Ray's work: one might instance Apu's decision to marry Aparna in *The World of Apu*, Doyamoyee's decision to return to her home and her doom in *Devi*, Mrinmoyee's decision to accept her husband in the second story of *Two Daughters*, and Charulata's decision to meet her husband on the threshold. It is not determinism: there is always the sense that conscious factors play a part in the characters' decisions, that they have an awareness of choice and the ability to make it. But neither is the choice entirely free: a whole complex of circumstances and influences contributes to these decisions, which we are never invited to explain in simple terms.

Pather Panchali ends with the family's departure for Benares. A long snake crawls through the rubble of the yard and over the cracked stone of the porch into the house. Nature is reclaiming what man had temporarily usurped and will eventually obliterate his traces. But Apu's part survives within him. As the ox wagon takes them toward the train, we see the mother lost in grief, unseeing, the father staring blankly back. But Apu is looking out with open, alert eyes at his past, as he will henceforth look toward his future.

APARAJITO

The first shots of *Aparajito* depend for their emotional effect partly on our having the end of the previous film clearly in our minds: the camera is inside a train crossing a huge bridge, through the metal struts of which we see the Ganges. The backward look from the ox cart that closed *Pather Panchali* is now turned toward the future—toward Benares, across the river, at which we are looking through Apu's eyes. The struts rhythmically flashing past communicate a sense of confusion and excitement and blur the view, but beyond them lies a great openness. The visual opposition of the open and the enclosed is one of the film's dominating motifs, suggestive of an indefinite "open" future from which Apu may be barred.

Aparajito is in its thematic-narrative structure the simplest of the three films and demands the least detailed treatment. The first section shows, in a series of individually vivid, loosely connected incidents, the life of the family in Benares and Apu's experience of the new world into which he is suddenly plunged; it ends with Hari's death. The film then gradually resolves itself into a prolonged and painful conflict between mother and son.

The Ganges.

Sarbojaya takes Apu back to the country (but not the same village as in *Pather Panchali*); he goes to school, and his yearning for knowledge and growth finds clearer direction; he grows up (the actor changes) and wins a scholarship for the college in Calcutta. But he is all Sarbojaya has left to live for. Apu struggles against her attempts to hold him back and progressively neglects her, but he is only finally released by her death.

Considered independently, *Aparajito* is the least completely satisfactory of the three films. There is the problem of the change-over of actors: the teenage Apu (Sumiran Ghoshal) doesn't look much like the child (Pinaki Sen Gupta, as in *Pather Panchali*). He looks even less like Soumitra Chatterjee, which creates a further

Hari prays.

problem of adjustment if one passes straight to *The World of Apu*. (Ray apparently considered Chatterjee for the role in *Aparajito* but decided he looked too old.) The difficulties here are superficial and scarcely insurmountable: they are of the kind about which a director surely has the right to invite us willingly to suspend our disbelief. Rather more serious is the way in which the manner and method of the film change halfway through: the first part is organized episodically in the manner of *Pather Panchali*; the second half is built on a single straight line of narrative, more like *The World of Apu*. The construction makes sense when one puts *Aparajito* back in its context, its center (where the structural change occurs) then becoming the midpoint of the whole trilogy.

This makes it the more surprising that Ray did not apparently plan to make *The World of Apu* when he was working on *Aparajito*: his second film, slightly disappointing as a sequel to *Pather Panchali*, is more than adequate considered as a transition to *The World of Apu*.

The opening scenes are likely to appear rambling and inconsequent to spectators who haven't seen *Pather Panchali*: a series of apparently random incidents showing Apu's experience of his new "world," in which the only clear narrative threads are Hari's job as prayer caller on the steps to the Ganges and his progressive weakening and illness. The randomness is necessary and expressive: we are presented with the child's experience of unconnected happenings, some of them beyond his understanding, which his developing consciousness must somehow assimilate. The principle that unifies this part of the film is the opposition of Apu's openness to new experience and his parents' enclosure. Up to the time of Hari's death, we never see Sarbojaya outside the family's apartment. It is Apu who is sent shopping, Apu who is sent upstairs to borrow matches from a neighbor; Sarbojaya is imprisoned in her role as wife and mother, washing floors, preparing meals, driving away intruding monkeys. This is a "social comment" on the position of women in Indian society, no doubt. But one feels also that it is in part a voluntary imprisonment, that Sarbojaya is trapped not only within the apartment but within her own limited mental attitudes: right up to her death, her instinct is to shut herself away from anything she doesn't already understand.

Apu, on the other hand, we see outside nearly all the time; and when he is in, he is wanting to go out. His first appearance in

Apu goes to borrow matches.

the film—his face suddenly peering around a corner—reminds us of his introduction in *Pather Panchali*: the emphasis is again on the alert, watching eyes. The scenes in which he experiences the city—pursued by a gang of boys and escaping by scrambling under a cow; wandering along the Ganges steps, past various prayer callers and a strong man practicing with a club-shaped weight—magically convey the child's excitement and wonder at a strange new world. (Perhaps Western audiences become too simply identified with the child's viewpoint in these sequences—for Indian audiences, presumably more familiar with what Apu sees, the effect may be closer to the "double vision" of *Pather Panchali*.)

Apu's first appearance.

If Sarbojaya is imprisoned in her role as housewife, Hari seems imprisoned in his profession. Whereas Apu wanders freely, Hari follows a single daily route, from home to his base near the bottom of the Ganges steps and back, a long, hard, straight climb, looking neither to right nor left. It comes across as a logical extension of Hari's introversion in *Pather Panchali*, his unawareness of his environment, his enclosure in vague dreams of success as a writer. The move to the city effects no radical change in the outlook of either parent. In *Pather Panchali*, Apu turned to his father as a way toward knowledge and freedom; in *Aparajito*, Hari becomes for the child simply a part of the general spectacle. We see Hari reciting prayers on the steps, surrounded by spectators. Apu stands

Apu watches Hari pray.

listening for a moment, holding a toy windmill, then runs off to explore the great buildings nearby, the river, its boats, and the variety of people engaged in mysterious adult activities, of which Hari is now merely one. Apu's development throughout the trilogy is partly analyzable in relation to what he casts off, in terms both of people and of attitudes.

The scene in which Hari's illness is first revealed expresses the enclosure/openness opposition—a matter of states of mind as much as of physical environment—in a characteristically poetic juxtaposition of images. It is a feast night. The sky is lit by fireworks. Hari returns home; Sarbojaya is lighting little flames within the apartment. She asks, "Couldn't we take Apu?" But

Hari feels faint on the Ganges steps.

Hari isn't well—he felt faint on the steps. We see him against the bars of a window, with fireworks shooting up outside in the darkness. Then Apu appears in the doorway holding a lighted sparkler. He is told he must stay with his father. He is learning English from a friend and practices: "Apu is a good boy." The sick man and the window bars; the night sky and the fireworks; Apu with the sparkler bringing the "magic" of the outside world into the apartment: the poetic movement finds its logical culmination in the boy's new learning, which goes beyond what Hari is equipped to teach him.

The scene of Hari's death and the sequences surrounding it are built of further juxtapositions of enclosure and freedom. We see Sarbojaya driving a monkey out of the apartment; the brief incident finds its "answer" in a scene following soon after Hari's death, in which Apu watches monkeys playing in a temple and feeds them. Here are two attitudes to environment: to the mother, the animals are a nuisance, to be excluded; to the child, they are a source of wonder and amusement, spontaneous wild creatures in the city, with which he feels a natural affinity. Hari is out at the river. He begins the long climb up the steps toward home and is called back: he has forgotten his spectacles. The incident hints at his growing weakness but also suggests his habitual inability to see anything outside him. A high-angle shot as he climbs emphasizes both the effort of the ascent and the straight line in which he moves. He collapses at the top of the steps and is carried home. The doctor diagnoses congestion of the chest; in fact, Hari will never leave the apartment again alive. Then there is a cut to Apu, outside: he is watching a full and dripping water bag being hauled up from a well. Then, with Hari ill and Apu out, the upstairs neighbor, drunk, tries to make advances to Sarbojaya; she drives him out with a kitchen knife. As Apu's life increasingly opens, his parents' lives become more and more closed. In the early morning, the dying father cries out for holy water from the Ganges. Apu goes down to the river, which is almost deserted. In the misty morning light, an athlete is practicing, and the child watches briefly. Ray intercuts this scene with Hari groaning as he dies, and registers the moment of death with a shot of pigeons flying up in great swarms, as if suddenly disturbed. The effect may strike one as somewhat rhetorical and self-consciously "symbolic" in a manner rare in Ray's work: it has been seen by an Indian critic as suggesting "the flight of the soul from the body."[5] It is more than this, however. Like the image of

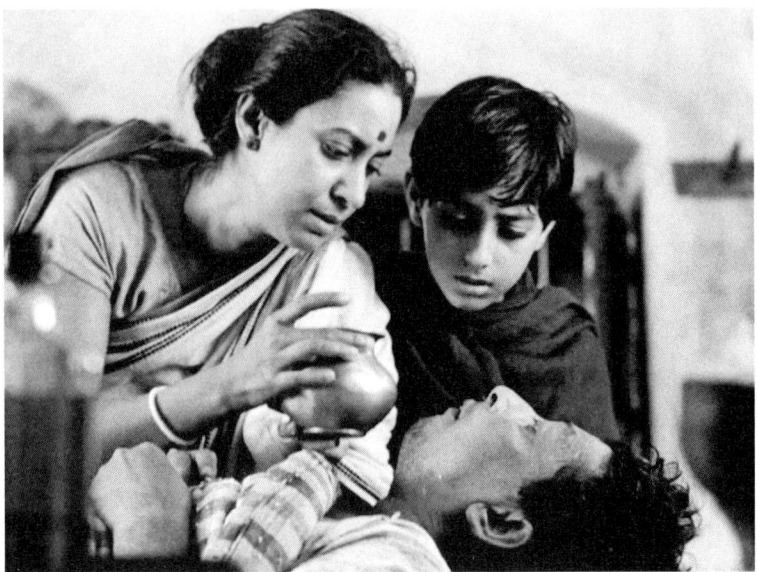

Hari dying.

the athlete exercising by the river in the morning light, it evokes a sense of energy and freedom in opposition to the progressively enclosed life of Apu's father; the image of the birds is as much triumphant as desolate, and it contradicts the sense of death at the same time as it expresses it.

Durga's death led to the move to the city; Hari's reverses this. Sarbojaya's decision to leave Benares for the country has as much claim to be considered the film's pivotal point as the more obvious one of the time gap during which Apu grows to adolescence. As usual, Ray doesn't spell out the motivation behind the decision, preferring to leave us with a sense that it grows out of the woman's whole life rather than from a single event. After

Hari's death, Sarbojaya gets work as a cook. When Hari's father comes, she is faced with a choice: she can accompany the family she works for to Dewanpur, or she can return with her father-in-law to his village. Even as her employer encourages her to go with them, Sarbojaya catches sight of Apu, hovering beyond some pillars, alone and neglected, waiting for her to be free. She decides; the next images return us to the opening of the film, yet in reverse, as we see the city from the train, disappearing from view, shut away beyond the struts of the bridge—Sarbojaya and Apu return with Apu's grandfather. On one level, Sarbojaya is sacrificing the new possibilities that were open to her in order to devote herself to her child: in the grandfather's village, she can become again simply a mother, and Apu will no longer be neglected. Yet the decision is also profoundly characteristic of Sarbojaya's psychology throughout and expresses her tendency to withdraw from life's challenges and novelties into the safe and the already familiar. In the name of motherhood, she is again voluntarily imprisoning herself and taking Apu into prison with her. When they arrive at the walled village in which they will now live, Ray gives us Apu's view of the train passing along the horizon in the distance, beyond the open fields; but he is within the gateway, which encloses the foreground of the image.

Of the three films of the trilogy, *Aparajito* is the one I least often feel an urge to return to. The episodic first part, though continuously touching, lacks the density of *Pather Panchali*; the remainder, built on a much straighter narrative progression, moves very slowly toward an inevitable outcome. But if this suggests failure, the film is one only in relative terms, viewed in the context of its neighbors. The justification for the very slow tempo is that

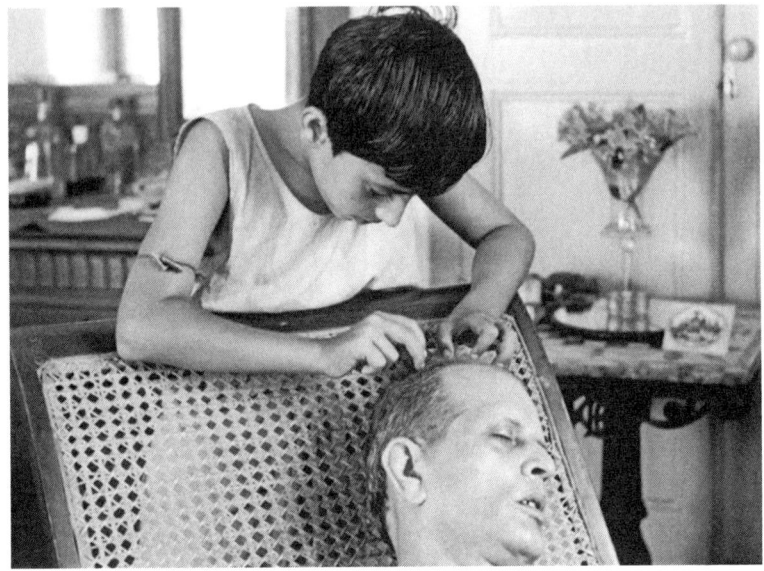

Apu also has work—searching for ticks.

Ray is not trying to *tell* us things but to communicate a total experience: the film invites us to steep ourselves in the characters' feelings and live through their conflict to its outcome rather than to take an intellectual "point." It invites rather than compels: the action is presented with Ray's customary objectivity, and our response is not forced on us. We are given time to enter fully into what the characters are experiencing, but it is essential that a certain distance be preserved, because the emotional force and complexity depends on the precise division of our sympathies between mother and son. This is one section of the trilogy (the sequences of Apu's wanderings after the death of Aparna in *The World of Apu* are another) that demands a certain deliberate exercising of patience from spectators brought up on the faster

Apu grows up.

tempo of the American cinema or the French New Wave, but the patience is amply repaid.

The universality of Ray's concerns is nowhere more evident. The film resolves itself into a conflict between the most basic needs of its characters: the need of the son to study, to learn, to widen his experience and reach out to a richer existence in which his potentialities can develop more fully; the need of the mother, widowed, with no one but Apu left to her and with no other resources—either inner or from outside—to give purpose to her life, to keep him with her. Successive scenes can scarcely fail to strike sympathetic chords in all of us, because the development of the situation is so closely related to universal experience: the scenes, for instance, showing Apu's delight in learning, his sense of personal triumph and of growing toward fulfillment, with at the same time his mother's feelings so delicately and sensitively conveyed: a woman torn between pride in her son's development and distrust of the very learning that will take him progressively further away from her.

The division of feelings within Sarbojaya is already evident in the scene in which Apu first expresses his desire to go to school. She is half pleased and willing to make the effort to cope financially, yet it is clear that she already senses his movement away from her into experiences beyond her grasp—senses it long before there is any *conscious* impulse in Apu to free himself from her. But the emphasis, in the early scenes of Apu's education, is on the child's delighted response to learning, and the freshness and immediacy with which this is conveyed is typical of the affirmative nature of Ray's art. Apu pleases an inspector and is praised by the headmaster, who tells him, "We live in a remote corner of Bengal, but we need not have a narrow outlook," and gives him books on Livingstone, Archimedes, Galileo, Newton. There is a tiny scene, handled by Ray with tenderness and humor, in which Apu tries to teach his mother astronomy, and Sarbojaya's face registers a whole complex of emotions: humiliation at her ignorance, pleasure in her son's knowledge, and that shrinking away from the unfamiliar that characterizes her whole development. And there is the magical and comic moment when Apu startles her by leaping out, dressed as a savage, with a cry of "Africa!"—assimilating by imitation, as he did in *Pather Panchali* when he made himself the silver-foil crown and moustache after watching the play. The simple incidents beautifully balance the typical and the particular, evoking all our childhoods yet suggesting the unusual energy and eagerness and sensibility of the young Apu. Our last glimpse of Apu the child is of him asleep at night over an exercise book, a single lantern burning beside him, the frail light driving back the surrounding darkness. The camera tracks in on him, and several years pass.

Apu's impulse toward fulfillment through learning thus firmly established, Ray moves at once to the decisive point in the conflict between mother and son. We see the headmaster addressing the adolescent Apu: he has the chance of a scholarship of ten rupees a month to study in Calcutta. He must ask his mother. The following sequences between mother and son, culminating in Apu's departure, are an admirable example of the balancing of distance and involvement, objectivity and sympathy,

Sarbojaya, Apu, and the globe.

that is the essence of Ray's art. He is never a "message" director: his allegiance is not to some given attitude so much as to the emotional truth, often many-sided, inherent in a total situation. The sequences could have been staged and shot so as to carry the meaning: "Son struggles for freedom against the attempted restrictions of possessive mother," or "Lonely, self-sacrificing mother is cruelly abandoned by thoughtless son." Either of these would imply a simple—and defensible—attitude toward life: the former a "pagan" belief in the supreme value of self-fulfillment and the necessity of casting off all that inhibits it; the latter a "Christian" belief in the supreme value of compassion and self-sacrifice. The construction and mise-en-scène of these and subsequent sequences of *Aparajito* make it impossible for us to see the action exclusively from either of these viewpoints. In this balancing of possible responses, both tragedy and optimism are implicit, a sense of realizable potentials coexisting with a sense of inherent and inescapable pain.

We see Apu and Sarbojaya in their home at night. He tells her he came second at school and goes on to mention the offered scholarship. As he mentions Calcutta, we hear the noise of a distant train softly on the soundtrack, with its opposed emotional associations for the two characters. Sarbojaya is hurt because he *wants* to go: "Who will look after me?" He tells her he doesn't want to be a "priest" all his life. "Your father was," exclaims Sarbojaya, and she slaps his face. Apu's remark, with its youthful brutality, its implicit contempt for Hari, partly deserves rebuke, but Sarbojaya's reaction is too extreme to be accountable for simply in terms of a desire to have her husband's memory honored. The response expresses her deeply conservative nature and, beyond it, her fear of loneliness. Apu's tactlessness, on the other hand, is partly excused by his sense of the need to fight for what he must have. At the end of the exchange, Ray unites the various components involved in a single shot: Sarbojaya is framed between the two posts of the doorway that enclose her; at her feet are the tokens of Apu's aspirations to a more open future, a book, his small globe, and the lantern. "We live in a remote corner of Bengal, but we need not have a narrow outlook."

Later, Sarbojaya goes out to find Apu and tell him he can go. From a box under her bed, she takes a bag of money: her savings from her work in Benares—the work, we recall, that she gave up in order to devote herself exclusively to her child. Apu reacts with unmitigated delight: his air of triumph affects us as at once moving (because it expresses an affirmation of life's possibilities) and cruel (because it leaves Sarbojaya's feelings entirely out of account). He shows her his globe, on which the camera tracks in. We next see the packing of Apu's case and his farewell. He is carrying his case and the globe—touchingly meager yet appropriate equipment with which to face the world of Calcutta and the future. Sarbojaya places a white spot on his forehead as he leaves (a blessing?). He walks away down the path without even a backward glance. As the camera tracks in on Sarbojaya, the smile of pleasure and pride fades from her face. She turns away and is last seen framed inside the doorposts, another image of loneliness and enclosure.

The remainder of the film alternates between the village and Calcutta. Apu attends college during the day, works for the "Royal Press" at night to pay his lodging, and falls asleep during a lesson on metonymy and synecdoche, supplying the lecturer with a convenient example of euphemism ("Not wholly attentive"). He and his friend are sent out and stroll by the river, talking of leaving on a ship. Apu says his mother would never agree to it: he is still tied to her, across the great distance, held back from the hypothetical future that the ship represents.

Then it is vacation time. Sarbojaya waits for Apu to come home. We see her by a pond, as a train passes across the distant horizon: two recurrent motifs brought together. The static pond, reminding us of that beside which Auntie stood in her final isolation, where Apu heard his father's agonized cries at the revelation of Durga's death, and into which he cast the stolen necklace; the train moving along with open horizon, with its associations of a freedom and potentiality from which Sarbojaya

Sarbojaya helps to pack.

is cut off; stagnation and development, the circle of enclosure and the straight line of liberation: Ray's simple imagery is rich in emotional connotation.

When Apu gets home—he has delayed his homecoming in order to work—the exchanges between him and his mother poignantly reveal the widening of the gulf between them. During his first meal, she asks him about food: does the cook in the city prepare food as well as his own mother? It is the one way in which she can compete, and she herself clearly feels its pathetic inadequacy. The question implies her total inability to grasp what is important to Apu in the life he is pursuing and her half awareness of this inability—of her exclusion from all those aspects of her son's life that are most significant to him. Then we see Apu reading in bed. Sarbojaya comes to his bedside—as if he were still a child—and makes him put his book away and tell her all he's seen. Mentally searching for something outside her experience yet within her grasp, he mentions cremations: the moment is a nice example of Ray's fusing of the poignant and the comic. Sarbojaya's response is, "I hope you're careful on the roads." She talks of illness and death, tells Apu she doesn't eat much. "I don't suppose you'd leave college to look after me?" But her son is already asleep.

The sequence showing Apu watching the local amusements—a man drumming, a boy walking on his hands—becomes more meaningful in relation to similar incidents in *Pather Panchali*. Apu the child discovered wonder in the most trivial events; Apu the young man, returned from Calcutta, views all before him with boredom. He turns away, walks to the river, pushes at a tree, half indolent, half frustrated; and he refuses to postpone

Apu reading.

his return to Calcutta in order to accept a local invitation. On the night before his return, he impresses on his mother that he must be called at sunrise to catch his train. At early morning, we see Sarbojaya leaning over him as he sleeps. The day before, she has treated him with bitterness and resentment; now, she looks down at him with tenderness. Asleep, he is her child again. But in the sudden horror with which she backs away, we see her realization of the falseness of this—her realization that as soon as he wakes up, she loses him again. He awakes and sees nothing of the intense and conflicting emotions she is experiencing; he seems scarcely aware of her existence; he is merely furious because it is late. Apu's surface indifference here makes all the stronger the sense of deep ties conveyed by what follows. Ray crosscuts between Apu at the station, buying his ticket and sitting on the platform, and Sarbojaya, leaning disconsolately against the post of the porch with the noise of the coming train in the distance. We see the train arrive. Ray cuts to Sarbojaya looking up: Apu returns and tells her he missed the train. He'll go tomorrow.

What emerges from these scenes above all is the sense of *necessary* tragedy: for Apu to sacrifice his future would be at least as tragic as for his mother to be abandoned. Destruction is necessary to creation, the two forces eternally interlinked.

And so comes the last "act" of *Aparajito*. Ray succinctly recapitulates the main elements of Apu's life in Calcutta—a

Apu's boredom while at home during his vacation.

montage of lessons, the press, Apu with his friend looking at ships. Then there is an exchange of letters. Apu reads his mother's: "Why do you write so seldom?"; he answers, evasively, that he has no holidays, his exams are next month. We see Sarbojaya holding his letter in her hand, her eyes dark and heavy. Ray's simple poetic images—simple in themselves, emotionally complex in the connotations they carry—are nowhere more beautifully used than in these closing sequences. Sarbojaya, as she dwindles toward death, becomes associated with a great majestic tree beneath which she sits apathetically, awaiting the son who never comes but who is now her only reason for existing. The woman's life has become little more than a matter of vegetable growth—or vegetable decay—except for our sense of continuing deep hurt that makes further striving meaningless. The flourishing, inanimate tree that has its "meaning" in just physically existing; the dying woman sinking into some subhuman state as her "meaning" is lost: the poetic juxtaposition takes on further overtones when Ray shows us Apu reading a book under a similar tree on the grounds of the college, an image that at once links and contrasts him with his mother.

We are returned to the village and to Sarbojaya by means of a shot of a sundial that Apu made during his early schooldays—evoking at once the past when he and his mother still lived in harmony and the learning that progressively separated them. Darkness falls. The camera slowly tilts down the tree to show Sarbojaya beneath it still; a train passes along the dusky horizon in distant silhouette. Sarbojaya goes into the house. A wick is burning low in the oil. She hears a sound, thinks it's Apu returned to her. The sequence of images recapitulates that of

APARAJITO

Sarbojaya sits apathetically beneath the tree.

Apu's previous homecoming; only this time the mother remains alone, as the shadows of night close in.

At last Apu gets a letter telling him of his mother's illness, and he leaves for home. After the "false" homecoming comes the real one: he walks along the familiar path, is met by a barking dog, passes the pond, and enters the enclosure, framed for a moment in its doorway. The emotional effect of the scene depends on the familiarity of each motif. He meets his grandfather and understands without need of words that Sarbojaya is dead. He sits under her tree and weeps. The camera tracks back until he is in long shot, leaving a great open space to the left of the frame, in contrast to the tighter framing of the earlier images of Sarbojaya in the same position.

But Apu is *aparajito*, the unvanquished; the film's last moments show his triumph—a very muted triumph—over grief and guilt. His grandfather urges him to perform his mother's last rites and then to become a holy man like his father. Apu doesn't commit himself verbally, but we next see him packing his bundle: he is returning to Calcutta. "I've got my exams," he tells the old man. And Sarbojaya's funeral rites? He'll perform them in Calcutta. The divided response that the film repeatedly evokes is felt again here, the spectator torn between a sense of Apu's brutality toward the past and his mother's memory and a sense of the necessity to push straight ahead on his path, rejecting hindrances that serve no useful purpose whatever their pulls in terms of sentiment. The grandfather is left framed in the doorway of the enclosure as Apu walks off along the open path toward the train—toward Calcutta. The camera tilts up to show the sky, Apu remaining within the frame in the lower part of the image. Each film of the trilogy ends with a new beginning.

THE WORLD OF APU

After *Aparajito*, Ray made two films unconnected with the trilogy, *The Philosopher's Stone*, a comedy, and *The Music Room* (*Jalsaghar*). He has said that he had no definite intention at that time of making *The World of Apu* but was persuaded to do so later. The film shows no sign of such reluctance. Far from suggesting any lack of inspiration or commitment on the part of its director, it is the crowning achievement of the trilogy, and (with *Charulata* and *Days and Nights in the Forest*, of those I have been able to see) one of Ray's finest films. The technique of *Pather Panchali* and *Aparajito* is never less than adequate to Ray's expressive needs, but in *The World of Apu*, the customary sensitivity and emotional delicacy are joined by a sense of greater assurance, both in the construction of the scenario and in the shooting and editing. There is nothing here of the hesitancy that somewhat detracts from the impact of *Aparajito*, no uncertainty of the direction in which the film is moving, and individual sequences have a greater compactness and force than anything in the earlier films. From *Pather Panchali*, Ray has always been a consistently sensitive director of actors, and it is difficult to think of a performance that is less than excellent in his films; but something of the strength of *The World of Apu* doubtless derives from the fact that it introduces for the first time in Ray's films two of his favorite players, Soumitra Chatterjee and Sharmila Tagore, familiar figures in a number of his subsequent works. In *The World of Apu*, their beauty—at once physical and spiritual—seems the ideal incarnation of Ray's belief in human potentialities. It is surely one of the most moving films ever made.

To talk of the "beauty" of Ray's protagonists is dangerous—the kind of thing his detractors crinkle up their noses at, suspecting that one is being precious or "aesthetic" or sentimental—but it is also inescapable. Ray shows no interest in evil characters—indeed, *is* there one in his films? There are many harmful actions, but they are almost invariably performed in good faith: one thinks of the father's sanctification of his daughter-in-law in *Devi* under the delusion that she is a goddess incarnate. There is also weakness: the son's inability effectively to oppose his father in the same film, or the vanity that prompts Amal to encourage Charulata to fall in love with him. The tragic tone is frequent in Ray's films, but the tragedy results from weak or misguided rather than deliberately malicious actions (the only exception I know of is the assault on Hari in *Days and Nights in the Forest*). There are no Gonerils and Regans in his work, nor even a Macbeth. This doubtless constitutes a limitation, but, as is usually the case, the limitation helps to define the qualities for which one values him.

Ray in the Apu trilogy is concerned centrally with events so basic and universal that to some the films appear simplistic: birth, death, marriage, the family, parenthood. This does not mean, however, that his characters are at all ordinary. On the contrary,

THE WORLD OF APU

Soumitra Chatterjee and Sharmila Tagore in *The World of Apu*.

he is concerned almost exclusively with exceptional people. This is already apparent by the end of *Pather Panchali*. The little boy who throws Durga's necklace into the pond is no "ordinary" child but a child of exceptional sensitivity and insight. When, in *The World of Apu*, Aparna's mother sees Apu as the God Krishna and his friend Pulu adds, "complete with flute," irony plays a part in the effect, but only a small part. Ray cuts to a shot of Apu, from a slightly low angle that emphasizes his stature, standing with a shy, pleased, half-embarrassed grin. He is at once very human and very godlike, naïve and immature, but illuminated by an inner grace. Can one speak of "idealization"? Both yes and no. In terms of potentialities—sensitivity, intelligence, the quality of aliveness, the ability to develop—Apu clearly embodies a human ideal. At the same time, Ray never sentimentalizes him. The character is clearly grasped and held in focus, at every moment, *as* a character with human shortcomings and weaknesses, tendencies to egoism and fecklessness. False idealization is always the product of the little man trying to be big; he presents a sentimentally idealized figure whom he doesn't understand, because he is too small to understand. Such an artist always betrays himself by his tone: his work becomes pretentious and strained; we are aware of rhetorical gestures and an underlying emptiness and unreality. Ray's films are entirely devoid of pretentiousness, and the rhetorical gesture is almost entirely foreign to them; his characters, "ideal" or not, remain intensely real. We feel we can trust him in his presentation of a human ideal: he understands his people intimately and can move freely among them because he exists on their level. The finest qualities of Ray's characters are those perceptible in his own films: while watching them, one feels in the presence of an exceptionally kind, generous, warm and sympathetic human being. If Apu is an "everyman" figure, it is in the sense that he embodies what is finest in universal human potentiality: he is ourselves, and he is the God Krishna made manifest. This is the essence of Ray's "humanism."

T. F. Powys wrote in one of his novels (*Unclay*) that "in every good book a light shines, that compels the reader to be joyful."[6] Powys is a very unfashionable novelist, and this, in these days of Joseph Losey and Roman Polanski and *M*A*S*H*, is a very unfashionable remark. But I believe it to be true. I don't know exactly what Powys means by the "light"; for me, it has nothing to do with whether the work in question is comic or tragic, whether it has a happy or sad ending. The "light" is that striving of the artist's being toward the establishment of standards for human life—toward as complete an understanding of life's potentialities as possible. It shines with uncommon strength and consistency in the films of Satyajit Ray, and there is a sense in which even the most tragic moments of his films, even as they evoke in us the profoundest sense of sorrow, at the same time "compel the viewer to be joyful."

Even quite minor characters in Ray's films are often granted a grace or dignity beyond the demands of their function in the plot. Consider the little scene near the beginning of *The World of Apu*, in which Apu is visited by his landlord, who has come to demand the long-overdue rent. Apu is shaving. The landlord sits down and asks Apu to give him a straight answer to a straight question. But the man is gentle and reasonable, though firm: the crucial demand has to be led up to ("What date is it?" and so on). When the demand for the rent comes, Apu says disarmingly, "That's *three* questions. It's not fair," and there is a momentary pause while the two men exchange smiles. It's impossible to do justice in print to such a moment, which in description sounds quite negligible. But something of the essential spirit of Ray's art is contained in it: there is the sense of communication and mutual understanding between two human beings who are not, after all, on intimate terms with each other; there is the exactness and clarity with which the landlord is presented, so that within this one brief scene, we have the sense of knowing him as an individual. His smile shows appreciation of Apu's charm and youth; but the landlord is not self-sacrificing and has no intention of withdrawing his demand. "Who are you to talk of what's fair?" is his response: Apu is not only occupying his room but using his electricity. When the landlord leaves, Apu switches on the entirely superfluous light before choosing which of his few precious books he will take to sell. The obvious way to do the scene would be "Apu victimized by nasty landlord." In fact, our responses are very precisely balanced so that we register Apu's action as immature and unreasonable, while it also implies a sense of values beyond the landlord's imagination.

The greater economy and force of Ray's style in *The World of Apu* is evident if one compares the introductory scenes of Apu's life in Calcutta with their equivalents in the first part of *Aparajito*. The first shots (apart from the brief precredit scene that shows Apu leaving college because he can't afford to continue and being urged by his teacher not to give up his writing) establish simply and vividly the material facts: a dirty curtain made of a rough sacking, with a large hole in it; rain blowing in; Apu asleep on the bed, dirty and unshaven; train noises from the railway yard outside. Apu is awakened by a train whistle. He goes outside onto the roof on which his garret opens, washes in the rain, performs his morning exercises. Ray cuts to long shot, so that the image frames the door to the garret (left), the open space beyond the roof parapet where the trains blow smoke and noise, and the young man exercising in the pouring rain, an image at once comic and touching, balancing a healthy resilience against a discouraging environment. The train imagery points us back through the trilogy, to that scene early in *Pather Panchali* in which Apu first becomes aware of the alien noise in the night, allowing us to feel the complexity of Ray's attitude to "progress": the trains,

Apu decides which books to sell to pay the rent.

once magical objects of wonder, are now commonplace, a part of the city's squalor.

Against this material environment, Ray sets Apu's attempts to find work. His qualifications are too good for the only teaching post available ("Would you work for ten rupees a month?" his interviewer asks rhetorically), and he recoils from the dehumanizing monotony of factory work. Meanwhile, he has received a letter from a magazine accepting one of his stories. It is clear that, without conceit, Apu is instinctively aware of his exceptional potentialities. The brief moment without dialogue when we see him shrink from the room where workers are sorting heaps of industrial glass objects allows us a characteristically complex response: we feel Apu's impracticality, his inability to come to terms with the tough realities of his environment, but we also register the recoil as evidence of his completely valid sense of his own potential, which the committing of himself to such work would limit and perhaps destroy.

"Visual poetry" is a term often used vaguely to mean "anything the viewer likes the look of." Applied to Ray, its meaning becomes more precise. Again and again in *The World of Apu*, one comes on scenes the emotional effect of which arises from the juxtaposition of components that have no precisely definable symbolic value but which in conjunction produce a resonance that verbal explanation, with its necessarily cruder emphases, risks distorting. After Apu's search for a job, he returns by bus, rereading the letter accepting the story; then he walks home along the railway track, where small pigs scavenge for food. The sun is setting behind the bridge; children are playing amid the smoke and dirt. The scene balances squalor and beauty, discouragement and hope, with Apu and his precise situation as focal point. The little scene that follows, again without dialogue, beautifully expresses Apu's sexual timidity and inexperience. He lies on his bed; across the yard, in a lighted room on the same level, a girl is standing by her window. Apu gets out his flute and closes the shutter: the girl moves away. She plays no role in the film, but a subtle sense is established of their awareness of each other, Apu's sensitivity to her presence expressed through his very shyness. The structural tautness of the film (again in comparison with the first part of *Aparajito*) is exemplified in what immediately follows: close-up of Apu on the bed playing his flute; the camera tracks back (as so often in Ray at moments that seem an intrusion into the characters' privacy) to show him in the wretched, dingy room; there is a rattling at the door. It is his friend Pulu, through whose agency (both direct and indirect) Apu later marries Aparna.

Apu's decision to marry Aparna is a crucial point in the film's narrative structure and at once the best example and vindication of Ray's method in the trilogy. Provided we are willing to make the necessary imaginative adjustment to a society (regarded by Apu himself as very retrograde—"Are we still living in the Dark Ages?") in which marriages are arranged with bride and groom not even introduced and in which the bride is considered cursed and henceforth ineligible if she isn't married at the time

Apu with his friend Pulu.

appointed, then we accept Apu's decision without question. Yet on the surface, it is a very strange and abrupt decision. Ray refuses to make things simple by having Apu tell us why he decides to marry Aparna: this would be to falsify not only our sense of complex motivation but Apu's, for it is clear that no simple explanation could possibly be adequate. What we feel is a density of implication, the decision evolving out of a web of interacting motives and promptings. It also makes the structure of the film appear tauter than we realized while watching it: to answer the question "Why does Apu marry Aparna?" is to reconstruct virtually the whole film up to that point. The nearest parallel I can think of in Western cinema is Dunson's decision not to shoot Matthew Garth at the end of Howard Hawks's *Red River*, behind which lies a similarly dense accumulation of implicit motivation. But certain films of Roberto Rossellini, as I shall suggest later, provide interesting comparisons.

One obvious factor in the background to Apu's decision is his aloneness. In the early scenes of the film, he had even cut himself off from Pulu, leaving no forwarding address when he changed lodging. His only contacts seem to be casual ones—the visit from the landlord, the brief exchange with the man of the same surname downstairs, who received Apu's letter by mistake. The aloneness is deliberate but appears to be motivated partly by shame at being penniless and living in a dilapidated garret.

Pulu—Apu's best friend and Aparna's cousin—exerts the strongest influence on Apu's decision at conscious level. Older than Apu, stable, intelligent and cultured, a protective elder-brother figure, he is also a link between not only the two characters but the two worlds, sharing Apu's educated outlook but tolerantly accepting the customs and superstitions of his rural relatives, sensitive to the fineness of their traditional culture, as Apu, with his much more primitive background, cannot be. It is he who persuades Apu to accompany him to Aparna's wedding, describing the delights of the country very much from the viewpoint of the wealthy to whom nature is a pleasing spectacle: a view on which our memories of Apu's childhood confer a certain irony. The importance to Apu of Pulu's opinion of him is evident at several points in the film, most strikingly in the scene on the boat as they travel upriver to the wedding. Apu plays his flute and declaims poetry while Pulu finishes reading Apu's (unfinished) novel. Pulu closes the manuscript and silently holds out his hand to Apu, then tells him the novel is wonderful. The intensity of Apu's pleasure at his friend's praise belies his previous seeming indifference.

Earlier, as Apu and Pulu walk home at night along the railway lines, in the darkness under the bridge, Apu describes the novel, and Pulu teases him: "It's not a novel. It's an autobiography." Apu admits the autobiographical elements but insists the book is more than that: it's written as fiction, it has a love interest. Again Pulu laughs: what does Apu know about love?—he's never got near a woman in his life. We recall the little scene when Apu closed his shutter to exclude the sight of the girl opposite and the scene even earlier when his downstairs neighbor, the other Mr. Roy, said how nice it would be to open a love letter by mistake, and Apu retorted, "No hope of that." In fact, Apu's diffidence with women is implicit in the childhood and adolescence shown in the two previous films. His father was away from home during much of Apu's childhood, an ineffectual dreamer from whom

Apu inherited his sensitivity and intellectual aspirations but also his inability to cope effectively with the world; and Hari died when Apu was still young. The dominant influences on his life were Durga and Sarbojaya. Women to Apu are his mother and sister: he doesn't know how to approach a girl on other terms. The presence of a "love interest" in an otherwise autobiographical novel suggests, however, his sense of unfulfilled needs, and Pulu's gentle teasing clearly disturbs him. The offer of Aparna—whom Apu has never met and doesn't have to court—is from this point of view a miraculous solution to the problem, and his acceptance of her is rooted deeply in his personal psychology.

In the scene with Pulu under the railway bridge, Apu reveals his touchingly naïve youthful pride in himself: he talks of the great novelists, Dostoyevsky, Lawrence—"and Apu Roy," Pulu cuts in with kindly irony. We realize that Apu, with a vanity altogether charming in its obvious vulnerability, does indeed see himself in that light. Just before this, elated by Pulu's company and the dinner he has been treated to, Apu declaims poetry up on the bridge until interrupted by a policeman who wants to know his name. "I am Mainack, son of Himalaya, mourning the loss of his wings," Apu declaims in answer. And Aparna's mother sees him as the God Krishna. Apu is exactly at the stage in his development to accept such a role. One of the functions of a god is to save: in agreeing to marry Aparna, Apu is performing a godlike action. "I felt I would be doing something noble to agree to it," he confesses to Aparna afterward.

All these factors can be felt to contribute to Apu's submission. They are unlikely all to be consciously present in our minds any more than in Apu's, but their background presence, interacting to predispose Apu to acceptance, subconsciously helps *us* to accept what might otherwise appear arbitrary. The mise-en-scène of the sequences leading to Apu's decision is carefully organized both to make the decision convincing and to suggest, mysteriously, that Apu is in some way to be involved in the wedding, before there is any question of his being the groom. From the scene in which Apu is welcomed by Aparna's mother, Ray moves us at once to the wedding preparations. Aparna, diffident and fragile, looking little more than a child, is being adorned and painted with the traditional bridal markings, while traditional Indian music is played. Then we see the procession of the groom (carried in a curtained and ornamented palanquin) approaching beside the river, accompanied by a band playing "For He's a Jolly Good Fellow," reiteratively and somewhat out of tune. The camera, keeping them in long shot, moves with them in a long tracking shot from the top of the bank. The river is in the background, trees intervene in the foreground, the procession passes between, at times almost disappearing from sight. Then, without a cut, the camera takes in Apu, lying asleep in the shade of the trees in the foreground of the screen, clutching his flute. The effect here is again achieved through poetic juxtaposition and suggestion rather than by anything one could call symbolism. The sequence juxtaposes three kinds of music—the traditional music associated with Aparna, the discordant bastard-Westernized music of the groom's band, and Apu's (silent) flute; and it juxtaposes the preparation of Aparna with a long take linking the groom and Apu and coming to rest decisively on the latter, sound asleep and quite unconscious of the possible involvement that the editing and mise-en-scène subtly imply.

When we next see Apu, he is lying in the same place, still asleep, still holding the flute, but dusk is falling. Meanwhile, Aparna's little potential tragedy has been succinctly expressed, the extreme economy intensifying the poignance. The groom's condition is shown in a single static take, the camera inside the palanquin so that the foreground of the screen, in which the groom plucks insanely at the floral headdress, traditional in Indian weddings (and which is to become a recurring motif in the film from here on), is enclosed in darkness. In the center of the screen, in the sunlight outside the palanquin, framed by its looped curtains, concerned figures come and go, including Aparna's father. Then, in a bedroom of the house, we see the mother holding the sobbing girl in her arms, shown at first in

Preparation of the bride: Aparna and her mother.

long shot but with an immediate rapid track-in that confers great intensity on the moment. The father stands in the doorway arguing helplessly that the wedding should continue; Pulu hovers in the background. The mother, furious, turns her husband out. At the top of the stairs, outside the room, he sadly consults with Pulu: if the ceremony doesn't take place, Aparna will never marry.

It is at this point that Ray moves us back to Apu, asleep in the gathering dusk. Pulu's voice calls; Apu wakes up; the situation is explained to him; the two men argue. As they talk, we see some of the groom's followers straggling back along the shore in the background of the image, the emotional effect of the scene partly defined by the reminder of the earlier tracking shot, partly by Ray's keeping the various components of the situation present for us. Then, at the moment Apu becomes aware of them, we are shown the little delegation that has accompanied Pulu, a group of men standing half helpless, half expectant in the shadows, like a silent pressure being exerted on Apu. He stands apart, shocked but awkward, aware of failing to meet the demands of people to whom he is indebted—the demands, especially, of Pulu. "Are we still living in the Dark Ages?" he asks defiantly. The camera tracks back from him to take in the whole group: Apu keeps himself separate, but the camera movement links him with the others. Pulu makes him feel guilty: like Dewey Martin at the end of Hawks's *The Big Sky*, he accepts the marriage partly to regain the respect of his best friend. The group moves off; Apu is left alone by the tree, picking up his book and his flute, emblems of his elected solitude.

Darkness falls. We see Apu, in the foreground of the image, moving toward the house, dark and slightly ominous in long shot, blocking the skyline. His movements and expression are hesitant: his resolution has weakened, but he still appears undecided. On the soundtrack, we hear a baby's cries, from somewhere in the night; and the insane groom is being led home by his friends—Apu watches as they pass him. Then he goes on to the house and asks Pulu, "Can you really get me that job?" adding, "I'll need a shave." We never know the exact moment when Apu decides or what tips the balance. The baby's cries are felt as part of the scene's atmosphere, together with the deepening darkness, the river, the house; Apu makes no sign that he even hears them, consciously. Yet it is legitimate—given the habitual economy, care, and exactness of Ray's use of sound—to feel the cries as contributing to Apu's decision: they are an emblem of vulnerability, relating at once to the helpless young girl Apu has never even met and the child they may one day have together. Later in the film, when Aparna is dead and Apu lies on his bed in a state of emotional desolation verging on atrophy, the clock in the room stops, and he gets up, goes to the railway, and tries to kill himself. I mentioned earlier a possible comparison with Rossellini. There is a scene in *Europa '51* in which Irene (Ingrid Bergman), after her child has killed himself, talks with her cousin in his car. She says that perhaps her child's life had depended on a single gesture, a word spoken or left unspoken; the cousin tells her that the child's death resulted from a great complex of causes, the state of the world, the fact that he had been born into, and grown up amid, the war and its aftermath. Rossellini allows both points equal weight, hence by implication equal truth: the boy's suicide was the outcome of a whole life and background, of an only partially decipherable network of interacting factors, but if

Irene had laid her hand for a moment on his, perhaps it would have been averted. Similarly, Apu marries Aparna because a baby cries and attempts suicide because a clock stops ticking.

The cumulative effect of Ray's films is somewhat like that of Rossellini's—felt especially at moments when a decision is reached and the whole weight of the film sensed to be behind it. To ask, for example, why the couple are reconciled at the end of *Viaggio in Italia* is to reconstruct the whole film, very much as we have reconstructed *The World of Apu* up to Apu's decision to accept Aparna. (It can hardly be simple coincidence that the two Western directors with whom Ray has the closest affinities should both have been attracted to India, each making one of his greatest films there.) There is an important, though somewhat intangible, difference: in Rossellini's films, there is customarily a sense of ultimate mystery—a sense one has to call religious—that is lacking in Ray. In Ray's films, one feels that everything *could* be explained if we were able to collect all the evidence from the characters' backgrounds and personal psychology; in Rossellini, there remains always a sense of the unknowable, of something almost certainly inaccessible to human beings, so that however fully one explains an event, the account is never complete. Hence, the reconciliation at the end of *Viaggio in Italia* has something of the miraculous, despite the fact that the accumulated events of the whole film are behind it.

The central section of *The World of Apu* offers one of the cinema's classic affirmative depictions of married life. It could sustain comparison with *Sunrise*: the range of emotions through which the characters pass is more limited, but the sense of inner development from the moment when Apu and Aparna marry to the moment when he receives the news of her death provides as convincing a demonstration of the meaning and positive value of marriage as Murnau's film. The wedding itself, where the couple first confront each other (though they can't meet each other's eyes), is a touching starting point. Ray shows it, essentially, in a single shot. The camera is at first on Aparna, at this point still an enigma but docile and amazingly delicate. Then it moves left to show Apu, now wearing the floral headdress, his face strained and frightened, his elation at pleasing his friend Pulu evaporated. The two are at once separate, because never in the frame together, yet linked because of the continuity of the shot.

This sense of two people separate yet in some still undefined way linked is maintained throughout the next scene. It is introduced by a shot of the river at night; we then see Apu looking out from the window of the bridal chamber. The physical realities of time and place are always important in Ray's work and treated with consistent exactness and sensitivity. Here, the steady progress from the sunlight and dappled shade when the groom arrived and Apu slept under the tree, through the dusk and falling night when Apu reached his decision, to the dense darkness of the world outside the garlanded and lamp-lit chamber, both emphasizes the swiftness with which events have taken place and intensifies the emotional effect of each scene with its changes of physical atmosphere. Here, the sense of surrounding darkness contributes significantly though unobtrusively to the mood as the two young people, still afraid to look at each other, shyly sound each other out and decide the future. Apu paces the room; Aparna stands motionless by the bedpost. Her back is to him, and they are separated by the bed; but Ray keeps them both within

The wedding night.

the frame throughout most of the sequence. Although we see Aparna's face, she remains at first as enigmatic to us as to Apu. He questions her to find out what she expects of him, painfully aware of the kind of existence he would be taking her back to. "What did Pulu tell you about me?"—she knows he is an orphan. Apu talks of his father, his mother, his sister. Does she know he is a writer? She tells him she can only read Bengali, and he answers that that is what he is writing his novel in. She is smiling shyly, looking down. With a sudden recoil, he tells her he was forced into this marriage. Does she want to be married to a poor man? "Yes," she answers. It is our key to Aparna: the certainty and simplicity of the one word imply the clarity, intelligence, and strength that later sequences will confirm; it comes across as not meek submission but a genuine decision reached through intuition and insight. It evokes an immediate response in Apu: he will take her back to Calcutta, even if her father objects.

We see them arrive at Apu's tenement block. As they descend from the carriage, Aparna is carrying the groom's headdress: from here on, it will rest in the corner of the couple's room, a reminder of the very different world from which Aparna has been brought, a world of wealth, stability, and tradition that contrasts not only with the squalor but the sense of impermanence of Apu's tenement by the railway, with its constant background of train noises. In the room, Aparna looks out through the hole in the rag-like curtain, which was the film's first image after the credits, at the yard below, where a woman places a baby on a makeshift bed

The bride arrives at her new home.

and small pigs scuffle about. Apu has gone to tell the neighbors that they have arrived. Aparna sits on the sill and weeps; the camera, with a movement of characteristic reticence, tracks back as if to respect her privacy. Apu returns and finds her weeping. She smiles, denying that she's unhappy. The poignance of the scene derives from the emotional truth of both the tears and the happiness, the young girl's misgivings about the life before her and the resilience that is partly innate strength and partly born out of her developing feeling for her husband. Apu takes Aparna to present her to the neighbors on the stairs, a group of admiring women and children who look up at her as if she were a visiting princess, the woman from the floor below putting out her hand to touch her; again we are aware of the gulf separating Aparna's world from the one in which she is now to live.

The whole span of the couple's married life together is covered in the ensuing six sequences, some of them very brief. The first opens on the new curtain that has replaced the torn one over the window by the bed. We see during the scene other small items of tangible evidence of the change Aparna has made in Apu's life. Near the beginning of the film, Pulu rebuked Apu for having a stove in his bedroom; now the cooking is done outside, over a small coal brazier on the roof. Near it is a pot of flowers. The room is neat, and there is another potted plant on the windowsill. Indian conventions and censorship demand extreme reticence in the depiction of sexual relationships, even within marriage. Ray finds indirect ways of suggesting physical intimacy that are perhaps more eloquent in their restraint, delicacy, and tenderness than scenes of overt lovemaking. The alarm rings; Aparna gets up: Apu has knotted the end of her sari to the garment wrapped

The downstairs neighbor sews while the newlyweds creep upstairs.

Aparna weeps.

around him, and she has to pause to undo it. It is at once a lover's joke and a suggestion of physical union. Apu opens his eyes. His hand is by Aparna's pillow, and between his fingers, he discovers a hairpin. He looks at her outside the door preparing the fire; there is a corresponding shot of him from her point of view. She rebukes him for staring. The editing makes vivid the intimacy of their exchanged glance in contrast with the shots in the wedding scenes that kept both characters within the frame but stressed their emotional separateness, their inability to confront each other. Apu pulls out a packet of cigarettes from under his pillow; his wife has written a note on the inner flap: "Remember—one after each meal." He looks across—she is smiling at him. The simple details are used by Ray to suggest the couple's delight in each other, the sense of wonder each feels expressed in the interplay of tenderness and gentle humor. Aparna swats a black beetle, smashes coal with her bare hands; Apu brings his flute out onto the roof, plays it intermittently, stands watching her. Again the overall effect of the scene arises from poetic juxtapositions: the sound of the flute, the noise of the train whistles (continued on the soundtrack while Apu still has the flute to his mouth); smoke from the trains, smoke from Aparna's cooking fire; the intimacy, quiet happiness, sense of permanence of the couple balanced against the sense of instability in the environment.

The second sequence begins with Aparna doing her hair, her husband dissatisfied, guilty at the hardship he has forced on her. "Don't you ever repine against your lot?" he asks (according to the English subtitles). She doesn't understand the word "repine." "Aren't you sorry you didn't marry a rich husband?" She laughs and continues brushing her hair. "You're laughing!"—"No, I'm

Aparna repining.

crying," she retorts, playfully contemptuous. He says he'll go out and hire a servant. And who will pay? He'll get more private pupils. She tells him to get rid of the one he has already. And then what? "Then my poor husband will come home early, and I shan't repine anymore." The latter part of the scene is done in a long two-shot with both faces visible in profile; there is a beautiful sense of intimacy in the way Aparna looks at Apu, of thoughts and feelings arising within her and finding expression in the words.

The third sequence has Aparna alone in the apartment. The alarm rings—it is time for Apu to come home. She looks down from the parapet, then hides behind the entrance and blows up a paper bag, which she bursts in his face as he appears: she isn't "repining"! The small, frivolous detail conveys an essential aspect of the relationship: Aparna's very exact sense of her husband's tendencies to melancholia and self-recrimination, from which she startles him with tender-ironic ridicule. Then we see them eating: he eats while she fans him, and then the roles and positions are exactly reversed. This sense of perfect balance in the relationship is strengthened in the next brief scene, in which Apu teaches Aparna English. Previously the gain, at least in concrete terms, has appeared to be mostly his; now we glimpse the possible developments the marriage offers Aparna.

The next sequence opens with a scene from the sort of Indian movie Satyajit Ray *doesn't* make: artificial sets, crude trick effects,

Apu teaches Aparna English.

wild melodrama, magicians and monsters. Apu and Aparna are in the audience watching it. The movie sequence ends with a child surrounded by a protective ring of magic fire; the image dissolves to a cab's back window, which is the same shape as the screen, the cinematic flames merging into real streetlights—Ray's brief artistic testament, perhaps, succinctly defining his own position in relation to the commercial Indian cinema. Aparna rebukes Apu for the extravagance of taking a cab; he does it so that they can be alone. Aparna, we learn, is going to her family home to have their baby. Apu will have time to work on his novel again: he hasn't touched it since his marriage. "Do you blame me for that?" Aparna asks. "No, I bless you for it." He tells her he'll dedicate it to her; again she doesn't understand what the word means. "To my wife," he murmurs dreamily, in English. She exclaims proudly that she knows what "wife" means. He tells her gravely that she doesn't—*he* does. She lights his cigarette and watches the match burn down, suddenly quiet and serious. The content of the scene is simple, and matched by the simplicity of the staging, but the overtones are complex. First, the screen in the cinema, which the couple are watching, becomes the window looking out on the world, from which they are turned away. The enclosed space of the cab they can't afford suggests the enclosed world in which they live, absorbed in their mutual fascination. To these unobtrusive hints is added the fact that Apu has suspended work on his novel. Suddenly the sense of the couple's relationship embodying an ideal is challenged, and we are returned to the recurrent assumption behind the trilogy that every gain is accompanied by loss (and vice versa). The value of the marriage is not in doubt, but it is now felt to have limitations, a tendency to shut out the wider reality beyond the couple's domestic life. The shortest and bleakest of Wordsworth's "Lucy" poems comes to mind:

> A slumber did my spirit seal,
>   I had no human fears.
> She seemed a thing that could not feel
>   The touch of earthly years[7]

And Apu's awakening is to be as abrupt, and as desolating in its effects, as that of Lucy's admirer. The match whose burning Aparna watches so intently subtly communicates the idea of transience. The delicacy of the scene's balance between poignance and gentle humor is beautifully maintained in its close. Apu, gazing at Aparna, her face lit by the match flame, asks romantically, "What is that in your eyes?" "Mascara," she answers and blows the match out.

The last of the six sequences shows Aparna's departure on the train. Close-ups of the two characters, faces strained with the grief of parting, are followed by an ominous low-angle shot of the engine, huge and black. The difficulty for Apu of facing even two months without his wife is vividly suggested and prepares us for the extremeness of his reaction to her death. The train, emblem of progress, link between primitive past and urban future, constant as a motif but repeatedly shifting in emotional significance, now bears Aparna away, and Apu never sees her again.

The sequence culminating in Apu's reception of the news of his wife's death in childbirth generates the most intense emotion of any scene in the trilogy; for the expression of a sense of irreparable loss, it seems to me unsurpassed in the cinema. The intensity arises mainly from the abruptness, expressed with shattering force in the mise-en-scène: the contrast between Apu's life with Aparna and life without her, compressed into a few seconds of screen time and communicated with an intimacy of feeling that is partly due to the directness with which the moment is presented, partly to the context of the whole film.

The scenes preceding the breaking of the news serve at once to intensify this sense of what the marriage means to Apu and to keep present for us the isolation of his life before it. We see him in the office where he now works, sitting dreaming beside his typewriter ("A slumber did my spirit seal . . ."). His coarser but amiable colleague says he wishes he knew Apu's secret: how to be married and happy on ten rupees a week. "How do you know I'm happy?" Apu asks, genuinely surprised. His colleague laughs kindly and feels no need to tell him. The motif that gives these scenes continuity is Apu's reading of a letter from Aparna. He takes it out in the office, as soon as he can feel private: "You owed me eight letters last month. I only received seven. I should never trust you, really." He is reading it again standing in the crowded train as he goes home: "jealous of the girl next door. Do keep the window shut." The line calls to mind the little scene in which Apu closed the shutter to exclude the girl opposite and makes suddenly vivid the difference in his life. He grins with pleasure and becomes abruptly aware of the presence of a fellow commuter staring at him in amazement ("How do you know I'm happy?"). We see him walking by the bridge (where he declaimed poetry after dinner with Pulu) and along the tracks (where he and Pulu discussed his novel, and Pulu asked him what he thought he knew about love), where he has the letter out again: "I am well but my heart is sick. It will heal if you come. If you don't, I shall never love you again, never, never...." They are Aparna's last words to him. He picks up a baby that has strayed too near the tracks, moving it back to a place of safety.

Aparna's brother is on the roof, standing where Apu stood with his flute as Aparna prepared the fire. He has difficulty in speaking. Apu moves toward him, with growing anxiety. The brother tells him that the baby came too soon. The camera tracks in on Apu's anguished face. We are used to Ray's camera withdrawing from his characters' moments of private emotion, moving back to frame them more "objectively" within the décor and as if to express a natural reticence and delicacy. The effect of the track-in is by contrast the more shocking. Apu's abrupt and unbelieving anguish is a difficult thing to ask an actor to convey; many directors would have found ways of covering up the precise moment of shock. Ray, with the always extraordinary Soumitra Chatterjee, gives it to us with uncompromising bareness and immediacy. Some people avert their eyes from details of violence or horror on the screen. The naked and hopeless suffering in this shot seems to me much harder to confront: it is among the cinema's most deeply shocking moments. The reality of death and irreparable loss has never been more sharply and painfully communicated. Apu turns briefly away and then abruptly strikes Aparna's brother, the futility and injustice of the gesture bringing home to us his impotence—*our* impotence—in the face of death.

This sense of powerlessness is intensified by the fact of the couple's separation. The scene on the roof is the culminating instance of the death-in-absence motif that runs through the trilogy. Hari's discovery of Durga's death was a moment of terrible desolation, yet a wife and son remained to him. The pain of Sarbojaya's death was counterbalanced by our sense of Apu's release. For Aparna's death, there is no immediate consolation or compensation—Apu being unable even to contemplate the existence of his child at this point—only an anguish made keener by the distance in space and time that places the girl beyond even an illusion of reach or help.

The sequences of Apu's marriage and Aparna's death are not only the core of this film but of central significance to Ray's work. They fuse, characteristically, the particularized and the universal. There is nothing vague or generalized about the characters and situations of *The World of Apu*. Ray realizes every stage in the couple's relationship in terms of precise and vivid detail that we respond to as neither "typical" nor "symbolic" but as fresh, interesting, touching, amusing in itself and for its own sake. The characters are presented with obvious affection that never degenerates into sentimentality because it is consistently balanced by a sharply focused objectivity. This particularity, however, is scarcely separable from issues that are universal: the intensity with which the particular marriage relationship and the individual death are felt and depicted point the spectator inevitably to marriage and death as facts of existence. More precisely, in terms of Ray's vision of life, the high value placed on the potentialities of marriage is challenged by the terrible unpredictability, hence potential absurdity, of an existence whose supreme value can be negated within a moment. The film's structure, in retrospect at least, highlights this sense of universality by framing the sequences of married life as the central panel of a near-symmetrical triptych, Apu's wedding and the news of Aparna's death dividing the film into three roughly equal parts, the formal organization giving the two events great prominence.

If Aparna's death, in its very arbitrariness, seems at first, both to Apu and to us, to render existence absurd, two factors on reflection qualify such a reaction and make possible the film's last third. One is the hint already implicit in the cab scene (after the cinema visit) that the perfection of the marriage in fact depended on attendant limitations—the exclusion of an outside reality, the suspension of Apu's creative work, emblematic of human aspirations whose continuance depends on the sense of incompleteness. The other is the fact scarcely acknowledged at this stage by Apu but present for the spectator in the words, at once cruelly tactless and realistic, of the neighbor who brings Apu food: "It's a good thing the child was saved"—Ray's sense of a universe of flux, of continual loss and gain, of a continuity in transience, a universe of which the "perfect" private world of Apu and Aparna was a living contradiction, is the basis on which will be built Apu's reconciliation with life and his acceptance of the child whose birth was Aparna's death.

It is striking that, while death plays so large a part in the trilogy, the spirit of the films seems quite free of morbidity. If one seeks a Western director in whose films death has a comparable importance—taking on a central thematic significance—one turns again to Rossellini (the comparison was suggested to me by Michael Walker). Again, both the similarity and the difference are illuminating. For Rossellini's characters, death—mysterious yet in human terms terribly final—is the ultimate test. There is no *natural* consolation—no compensatory gain in nature for the loss. The only gain arises from the way in which characters' awareness of death forces them to strive to create a meaning in their lives. The fact of death suddenly puts the individual life in a new perspective. Other concepts—the sense of the vastness and terrible splendor of the universe, the awareness of time and the brevity of the individual life in relation to eternity, perhaps the idea of God—are often inseparably bound up with the awareness of death. I am thinking of Ingrid Bergman's experience of the volcano in the last sequences of *Stromboli*; her reactions to the lovers immortalized in death in the Pompeii lava in *Viaggio in Italia* ("Life is so short"); the death of her child in *Europa '51*, from which all the developments of the film spring. Or there is the last shot of *La Prise de Pouvoir par Louis XIV*—the only shot in which we see Louis alone and which creates in a moment the essential significance of the whole film—in which Le Roi Soleil, after divesting himself of the clothes that symbolize the public role in which he has deliberately submerged his private identity, repeats the maxim of La Rochefoucauld, "Neither the sun nor death can be looked at unflinchingly." Every Rossellini film leads one, sooner or later, to his religious sense of mystery—not necessarily Catholic or even Christian, as one sees clearly if one compares his films with Robert Bresson's, which can only be understood in relation to Christian dogma.

For Ray, death is not so much a mystery as a terrible fact, something one has to learn to live with rather than a final judgment and challenge that abruptly and mystically changes one's whole perspective. Apu's development in the last third of *The World of Apu* is determined not so much by the fact of death (as would be the case in Rossellini) as by *Aparna's* death—by his sense of irremediable loss. And in the trilogy, although death remains terrible in its arbitrariness, there is always compensation in natural-human terms of development or continuity: Auntie dies, the children grow; Durga dies, the family move to Benares; Sarbojaya dies, Apu is set free to seek self-fulfillment; Aparna dies, the baby is born.

The inescapable comparison evoked by the last part of *The World of Apu*, it seems to me, is with the late plays of Shakespeare. The ultimate value comparison would have to be between Ray's mise-en-scène and Shakespeare's poetry, and the judgment would be predictable and not particularly interesting: when Ray made *The World of Apu*, he had not evolved anything equivalent to the extraordinary expressive flexibility and complexity of *The Winter's Tale*. Nonetheless, the comparison is very far from making him look ridiculous, and it suggests, I think, the level on which the film must be interpreted and valued: not as a sentimental tale of little-boy-finds-his-daddy but as a poem about rebirth and reconciliation. The parallels are striking, *Pericles* offering the closest. There is the progress through catastrophe and loss (the death of Thaisa, the death of Aparna) to final acceptance. There is the use of the child—renounced by the father, like Marina, but for more comprehensible motives—as both the agent of the protagonist's reconciliation with life and the symbol of rebirth through natural continuity. Shakespeare, in both *Pericles* and *The Winter's Tale*, resurrects the mother, too. Ray in a sense resurrects Aparna, with the aid of what looks like miraculous good fortune in the casting: the child who plays Kajal, the son, immediately evokes memories of the child Apu in his aliveness and sensitivity, but his physical resemblance to Aparna is perhaps even more striking—he has the same delicacy of features, the same large, vulnerable eyes. I find his appearance instantly moving in itself.

The turning point in Apu's progress from despair to acceptance is the attempted suicide on the railway tracks. The moment when Apu decides to kill himself is rendered with characteristic exactness of effect. Since Aparna's death, Apu has lain prostrate and virtually motionless on the bed. The well-meaning neighbor, Mrs. Ganguly, brings him food, talks about other possible wives for him, tells him it's a good thing the child was saved. When she leaves, Apu rises painfully. Ray cuts to a close-up of his face; the clock stops ticking; Apu turns to the mirror, and the camera turns to frame his reflection; we hear the sound of a train whistle. Each detail is presented simply, without overt comment: we are left to feel their power of suggestion, Ray moving immediately to the suicide attempt. For Apu, the suggestions are supported and given force by the memory of the past, and Ray makes the past present for us as well by subtle means of which the accumulated resonances of the train imagery constitute only the most obvious. The moment when Apu at last rises from his bed is shown in a shot in which the camera moves from left to right across the room, placing the action within the décor that includes the new flowery curtain Aparna made (at left center of the image when the camera stops moving) and the groom's wedding headdress in the corner at the right. When Apu looks at his reflection, Ray moves the camera in so that the mirror becomes a frame within the frame, recalling the earlier "frames" of the cinema screen and the cab window, the couple's last evening out together. The image within the frame is neither the crude fantasy melodrama nor the outside world but Apu's own haggard and unshaven face, his eyes revealing his despair as he looks within himself.

The emotional effect of the suicide scene is similarly deepened by Ray's use of motifs that have accumulated resonances from previous appearances in the film. What happens is simple: Apu stands beside the tracks, waiting to fall in front of an oncoming train; the train runs over a pig, whose death scream arrests Apu, so that he is still standing in the same place as the train passes. Ray shoots the scene in a manner that gives particular emphasis to two elements: smoke and the various sounds involved. The sequence starts with the camera tilted up to the sky. The image remains quite empty as we hear the whistle of the approaching train; then dark smoke appears from the bottom left of the screen,

Apu contemplates suicide by the passing train.

and the camera moves to take in Apu, in the right foreground of the frame. The effect is to deprive the image of all environmental context, the elimination of all but the barest essentials reflecting Apu's single-minded concentration on his death. In the scene of domestic life earlier, Ray juxtaposed the smoke from trains with the smoke of Aparna's fire, the noise of the train whistles with the sound of Apu's flute; here the train whistle is juxtaposed with the scream of the pig. The straying pigs were earlier in the film associated visually with children. Before Apu learned of Aparna's death, he removed a straying child from the railway tracks. The suicide scene draws together, by association, all these motifs, linking them by implication also with Aparna's death and Apu's child. There is nothing schematic or overtly symbolic, rather an effect of poetic density dependent on the keeping present in our minds the emotional resonances of past incidents.

The brief sequences showing Apu's wanderings and his immersion in nature seem to me the weakest in the film, substituting generalized, picturesque, rather obvious images—Apu gazing out to sea, Apu wandering through sunlit forests—for the closely observed particularities we are used to in Ray. In place of the precise and complex motivation, part expressed, part implied, behind the earlier stages in Apu's development, they offer little more than a romantic gesture. They culminate in what seems to me the film's most problematic moment—Apu's destruction of his novel on a mountaintop as the sun rises. The problem lies in assessing the precise tone of the scene. Apu, clearly enough, is casting off a past he has outgrown, the novel representing a level of experience and of achievement that he has left behind with Aparna's death and can now reject as immature. At the same time, there is something grandiose and rhetorical in the gesture, an act of self-dramatization that suggests a continuing immaturity: if one wishes simply to cast off one's outgrown past in the form of a novel, one needn't climb a mountain peak and cast the leaves into the sunrise. If one could be confident this were the point, the scene would be perfectly acceptable, establishing a transition stage in Apu's life: he is, after all, not yet ready fully to accept life and its conditions, in the form of the child for whose birth Aparna died. But Ray's filming of the scene—camera looking up at Apu from a low angle, giving him an almost saint- or prophet-like stature—seems to indulge the character's emotion unquestioningly. Ray himself sees the incident simply as an act of "renunciation" and suggests that "the Indian audience is familiar with a situation like that; it might seem strange to a Western audience": a justification that perhaps merely evades the real issue, though there may be a conflict here between the values accorded to certain emotional states and attitudes in Eastern and Western cultures.

Certainly, Apu's "renunciation" is not to be taken as a desirable absolute. When we next see him, we realize that he was renouncing more than the immature novel: he has rejected the whole creative and aspiring side of his nature and is working at a coal mine in Central India. At the beginning of the film, he shrank from factory work as a means of earning a living, a reaction at once immature yet suggestive of a genuine fineness of sensibility, a reluctance to get trapped in uncreative routine. Accordingly, the revelation of his mining work also evokes a mixed reaction. We see he has found through it a certain stability and peace of mind but at the expense of much of what was finest

Apu flings the pages of his novel from a mountaintop.

in him. His job isn't really a return to humanity: like his previous absorption in nature, it appears rather a rejection of his human sensitivity, his sensitive awareness of individual lives, after the pain of Aparna's loss. The destruction of the novel is clearly bound up with this. We know the novel was immature, a "young man's book"; we also know it was the expression of a very real and promising talent, for the intelligence and steadiness with which Ray invests Pulu give his opinion of it considerable weight. It is this side of Apu—the side of which the impulse to write was an expression—that must be restored to life.

Meanwhile, we have been introduced to the child, Kajal; with him, the delicacy and sureness of touch returns. The method of his introduction is as striking and instantly meaningful as the close-up of the opening eye that introduced Apu in *Pather Panchali*. We see first his feet; the camera moves up to show his hands, holding a catapult, then continues upward to show not the face but a grotesque devil mask, which he tips back over his head to reveal the face beneath, sensitive, vulnerable, intensely alive. In each case, Ray finds a way of communicating the essential characteristic immediately: with Apu, the enquiring eye looking out onto the world; with Kajal, the aggression that is really a defense against hurt in a world where, fatherless, he must protect himself. The images are linked by the fact that both children are hiding—Apu under a blanket, Kajal behind the mask; and they connect, too, with the introduction of Apu in *Aparajito*, suddenly peering out from his place of concealment round a corner. If Kajal's face recalls Aparna's, he is also his father's son, with the same balance of vulnerability and resilience, timidity and curiosity.

The implications of this first image of Kajal are developed in the incident of the dead bird. Kajal picks up the bird—which he seems to associate with his catapult, though there is no suggestion that he has killed it—examines it, and makes a face at it: his way of coping with the disturbing fact of death and his own possible guilt. Then he frightens an old woman by dangling the bird over her as she cooks, grabbing the food and running before she can pull herself together. He is caught by an old man, whom he promptly bites. The old man threatens to tell Kajal's grandfather; the child immediately retaliates with a counterthreat—"My father will hit you." We are left to make connections between the various bits of evidence—devil mask and catapult; the face-pulling at the bird; the childish delinquency; the apparent, almost reckless

Kajal, the mask, and the dead bird.

self-reliance; the sudden falling back on the myth of a father whom he has never seen and who has for him the reality of a character in a fairy story—and find a coherent pattern. However, beyond the psychological sketch of the child's response to his abandonment (we gather subsequently that the grandfather often speaks of Apu disapprovingly), Ray suggests the existence in Kajal of qualities that make him a fitting medium and symbol of the idea of rebirth and of natural continuity, the idea that nothing is ever simply lost. If the vulnerability comes from Apu, the practical resourcefulness and self-reliance are clearly a legacy of the mother: Kajal is, potentially at least, the fusion of what was finest in both his parents.

As Pulu led Apu to Aparna, so he leads Apu to his child. Pulu's function in the film, though less active and less developed, is not unlike that of Camillo or Paulina in *The Winter's Tale*: lacking Apu's fineness, he has what Apu lacks, a sturdy common sense and dependability. Having visited the grandfather (his uncle) and seen Kajal, he then seeks out Apu at the mine. In their interview on a hillside track, the qualities the two men embody are very nicely balanced: on the one hand Pulu's sense of decency and responsibility, on the other Apu's capacity for deep hurt and its attendant egoism. At first, Apu shrinks even from contact with his friend—contact that inevitably brings with it reminders of all he has sought to forget, deadening the sensitive side of his nature in the process. Warily, the two men draw near each other. Apu says he thinks of going abroad—a further flight, perhaps, from those aspects of himself that tend to human commitment. Pulu mentions Kajal. "Oh, so that's what they called him," Apu says: he has deadened in himself all response to the child's existence. Ray films the latter part of the conversation with Apu at the outer edge of the track, the sky and valley behind him. As the two men discuss Kajal, Apu is between two small trees growing out of the side of the hill, one alive and one dead; when Apu says, "She died because he was born," he sits, the dead tree behind him. Verbalized, the symbolism sounds much cruder than it is—in fact, it is never visually stressed by "significant" cut-ins or camera movements.

And so comes the closing sequence of the film and of the trilogy: Apu's visit to his father-in-law's house, where through a process of tentative but reciprocal communication, he moves from rejection of the child to joyful acceptance. He comes with

Pulu comes to find Apu.

the intention of coldly executing a parental duty: he is going abroad and will first leave Kajal in his own village to take him off the grandfather's hands. Apu goes upstairs to see his child for the first time. The scene is rich in unobtrusive but subtly suggestive poetic detail. Kajal is asleep on the bed, the devil mask lying beside him. Apu sits on a chair by the window, through which we see, in long shot, the river, with a solitary boat moving. From somewhere outside comes the sound of a voice singing, the only thing that breaks the silence. The river, besides it traditional overtones of "river of life," has something of the function of the railway in *Pather Panchali*: it is the way to Calcutta and the future. The voice, with its distant yearning quality, stands in for Apu's awakening feelings for the child, which it perhaps also helps to provoke, rather as the cry of a baby in the gathering darkness played its role in his decision to marry Aparna.

Apu awakens Kajal, who runs out. Apu follows him out of the house, through the gate, the grandfather hovering anxiously behind. "Kajal, I'm your father." The child's response is to hurl a stone, an action capable of several interpretations: anger at the father's previous rejection of him; reluctance to have a fantasy figure, a hero from a fairy tale, reduced to mere flesh and blood; the fighting off of the powerful and disturbing emotions that Apu's sudden presence arouses. Ray's inexplicitness allows us to sense complex interacting impulses behind the child's action. The grandfather makes to strike Kajal with a stick, and Apu physically intervenes. The moment is moving not only because it

Apu sees his son for the first time.

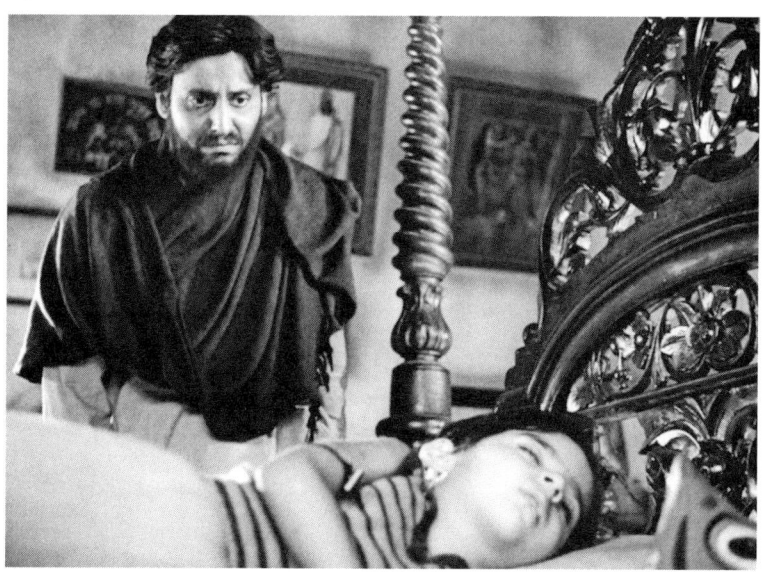

suggests the strength of the feeling for his son awakened in Apu but because it is the fulfillment of Kajal's fantasy about his father, an effective defense against the grandfather's punishments. (The staging of the scene is somewhat clumsy: Kajal seems too far away for the stone to reach Apu, a fact Ray tries to disguise in the editing; and the grandfather's and Apu's movements look too posed and unspontaneous. One could argue that Ray was trying to heighten the action by making it almost ritualistic, but such an effect seems at once superfluous and uncharacteristic. He never seems at ease in the treatment of physical violence: there is a similar weakness in *Days and Nights in the Forest*.)

The next two brief scenes both show Apu's advances rejected by Kajal; Ray's mise-en-scène, however, suggests the reciprocal nature

Kajal between his grandfather and father.

of the contact. In the first, we see Apu but not Kajal; in the second, a single static take, we see Kajal but not Apu (except his hand): the formal balancing suggests the connection that the child's actions deny. The first scene has Apu directing a clockwork train across the floor toward Kajal; it is immediately flung back at him. The second has Kajal in bed. We hear Apu's voice: "Will you make friends?" He offers to tell Kajal stories. Kajal says nothing: a sign perhaps that he is now ready at least to listen to his father's advances and consider them. But then Apu lays his hand on the boy's shoulder. Kajal is not ready for physical contact: the hand is firmly pushed away.

Apu prepares to leave. He won't compel the child to accompany him, although Aparna's father tells him he has the right ("I knew you'd turn out to be a failure," the old man grumbles).

Apu leaves as Kajal watches from a distance.

Apu carrying Kajal—an end and a new beginning.

We see Apu walking away along the riverbank where, earlier in the film, he moved hesitantly toward the marriage with Aparna. He pauses suddenly and turns as if arrested by some sixth sense. The shot is a marvelous example of the expressive possibilities of depth of focus: Apu in the foreground, left, in close-up, the tiny figure of the child in distant long shot, following, the two separated by a great space yet linked within a single composition. In the background is the river; we hear the sound of the wind and a repeated birdcall. Apu at first pretends not to notice Kajal, letting the child get nearer. Then, over the space that still separates them, Apu and Kajal discuss the child's father in the third person. It is clear that Kajal "knows" that Apu is his father but still can't quite accept the fact. He asks Apu if he knows his father. Apu says he does and offers to take Kajal to him. In the background behind Kajal, the grandfather appears to take the boy in, carrying in his hand the spurned clockwork train. He pauses, seeing what is happening. Apu urges the child on. Suddenly the boy relaxes and rushes forward into his father's arms. The film ends with him seated on Apu's shoulders as Apu walks away toward the future. In accepting the child, he has accepted life, has accepted the death of Aparna. Whether or not he is going back to become a great novelist is immaterial: he is going back to *live*.

NOTES

1. Folke Isaksson, "Conversation with Satyajit Ray," *Sight and Sound* 39, no. 3 (1970): 119.
2. T. G. Vaidyanathan, "Death in the Trilogy," *Montage* (Bombay) 5–6 (July 1966), unpaginated.
3. François Truffaut, *Hitchcock/Truffaut* (New York: Simon and Schuster, 1967), 42–43.
4. William Wordsworth, "Lines Composed a Few Miles above Tintern Abbey" (1798), in *The Poetical Works of William Wordsworth*, 2nd ed., ed. Ernest De Selincourt (Oxford, UK: Clarendon, 1952), 259.
5. Vaidyanathan, "Death in the Trilogy."
6. T. F. Powys, *Unclay* (London: Chatto and Windus, 1931), 149.
7. William Wordsworth, "A Slumber Did My Spirit Seal," in *Poetical Works*, 216.

FILMOGRAPHY

Pather Panchali (Song of the Road) (1955)
Director: **Satyajit Ray**. Production company: Government of West Bengal. Producer: **Satyajit Ray**. Screenwriter: **Satyajit Ray**, from a novel by Bibhutibhushan Banoyopadhyay (Bibhuti Bhushan Bannerjee). Cinematographer: Subrata Mitra. Art director: Banshi Chandragupta. Music: Ravi Shankar. Editor: Dulal Dutta. 122 min.

Principal Cast: Kanu Bannerjee (Harihar Ray), Karuna Bannerjee (Sarbojaya Ray), Uma Das Gupta (Durga, the daughter), Subir Bannerjee (Apu, the son), Chunibala Devi (Indir Thakrun, the aunt), Runki Banerjee (little Durga)

Aparajito (The Unvanquished) (1957)
Director: **Satyajit Ray**. Production company: Epic Films. Producer: **Satyajit Ray**. Screenwriter: **Satyajit Ray**, from a novel by Bibhutibhushan Banoyopadhyay (Bibhuti Bhushan Bannerjee). Cinematographer: Sabrata Mitra. Art director: Bansi Cahndragupta. Music: Ravi Shankar. Editor: Dulal Dutta. 113 min.

Principal Cast: Piaki Sen Gupta (Apu), Kanu Bannerjee (Harihar), Subodh Ganguly (headmaster), K. S. Pandey (Pandey), Karuna Bannerjee (Sarbojaya), Smaran Ghosal (Apu, the adolescent), Charu Ghosh (Nanda Babi), Santi Gupta (Ginnima), Ajay Mitra (Anil), Kamala Adhikari (Mokshada), Lalchand Banerjee (Lahiri), Kali Bannerjee (Kathak), Hemanta Chatterjee (professor)

Paras Pathar (*The Philosopher's Stone*) (1958)

Director: **Satyajit Ray**. Production company: Aurora, L. B. Films International. Producer: Promod Lahiri. Screenwriter: **Satyajit Ray**, from a story by Rajshekar "Parashuram" Basu. Cinematographer: Subrata Mitra. Art director: Bansi Chandragupta. Music: Ravi Shankar, **Satyajit Ray**. Editor: Dulal Dutta. 111 min.

Principal Cast: Tulsi Chakraborty (Paresh Chandra Dutta), Kali Bannerjee (Priyotosh Henry Biswas), Ranibala (Gribala Dutta), Gangapada Basu (Kachalu), Haridhan Mukherjee (police inspector), Jahar Roy (Bhajahari)

Jalsaghar (*The Music Room*) (1958)

Director: **Satyajit Ray**. Production company: Satyajit Ray Productions. Producer: **Satyajit Ray**. Screenwriter: **Satyajit Ray**, from a story by Tarashankar Banerjee. Cinematographer: Subrata Mitra. Art director: Bansi Chandragupta. Music: Ustad Vilayat Khan. Editor: Dulal Dutta. 100 min.

Principal Cast: Chhabi Biswas (Huzur Biswambhar Roy)

FILMOGRAPHY

Apu Sansar (The World of Apu) (1959)

Director: **Satyajit Ray**. Production company: Satyajit Ray Productions. Producer: **Satyajit Ray**. Screenwriter: **Satyajit Ray**, from a novel by Bibhutibhushan Banoyopadhyay (Bibhuti Bhushan Bannerjee). Cinematographer: Subrata Mitra. Art director: Bansi Chandragupta. Editor: Dulal Dutta. Music: Ravi Shankar. 105 min.

Principle Cast: Soumitra Chatterjee (Apu), Sharmila Tagore (Aparna), Swapan Mukherjee (Pulu), S. Aloke Chakravarty (Kajal).

Devi (The Goddess) (1960)

Director: **Satyajit Ray**. Production company: Satyajit Ray Productions. Producer: Aminyanath Mukherji, **Satyajit Ray**. Screenwriter: **Satyajit Ray**, from a story by Prabhat Kumar Mukherjee. Cinematographer: Subrata Mitra. Art director: Bansi Chandragupta. Music: Ali Akbar Khan. Editor: Dulal Dutta. 93 min.

Principal Cast: Chhabi Biswas (Kalikinkar Roy), Sharmila Tagore (Doyamoyee), Soumitra Chatterjee (Umaprasad), Karuna Banerjee (Harasundari), Pernendu Mukherjee (Taraprasad), Arpan Chowdhury (Khoka)

Rabindranath Tagore (1961)

Director: **Satyajit Ray**. Production company: Films Division, Government of India. Screenwriter: **Satyajit Ray**. Cinematographer: Soumendu Roy. Art director: Bansi Chandragupta. Music: Jyotindra Moitra. Editor: Dulal Dutta. 54 min.

Principle Cast: Sumiran Ghoshal (Tagore), Kallol Bose, Subir Bose, Norman Ellis, Sovanlal Ganguli, Pernendu Mukherjee

*Teen Kanya (Three Daughters
also known as Two Daughters)* (1961)
Director: **Satyajit Ray**. Production company: Satyajit Ray Productions, Calcutta. Producer: Aminyanath Mukherji, **Satyajit Ray**. Screenwriter: **Satyajit Ray**, from stories by Rabindranath Tagore. Cinematographer: Soumendu Roy. Art director: Bansi Chandragupta. Music: **Satyajit Ray**. Editor: Dulal Dutta. 173 min.

Principal Cast: "Postmaster": Anil Chatterjee (Nandal), Chandana Banerjee (Ratan); Nripati Chatterjee (Bishey), Khagen Pathak (Khagen), Gopal Sen (Bilash); "Monihara": Kali Bannerjee (Phanibhushan Saha), Kanika Majumdar (Manimalika), Govinda Chakravarti (schoolmaster and narrator); "Samapti": Aparna Das Gupta (Mrinmoyee), Soumitra Chatterjee (Amulya)

Kanchenjunga (1962)
Director: **Satyajit Ray**. Production company: NCA Productions. Producer: **Satyajit Ray**. Screenwriter: **Satyajit Ray**. Cinematographer: Subrata Mitra. Art director: Bansi Chandragupta. Music: **Satyajit Ray**. Editor: **Dulal Dutta**. 102 min.

Principal Cast: Chhabi Biswas (Indranath Choudhuri), Alakananda Ray (Monisha), Anil Chatterjee (Anil), Karuna Bannerjee (Labanya Roy Choudhuri), Pahadi Sanyal (Jagadish), Anubha Gupta (Anima), N. Viswanathan (Bannerjee), Arun

Mukherjee (Ashoke), Subrata Sensharma (Shankar), Indrani Singh (Tuklu), Vidya Sinha (Vidya), Haridhan Mukherjee

Abhijaan (*The Expedition*) (1962)
Director: **Satyajit Ray**. Production company: Abhijatrik. Producer: Bhola Nath Roy. Screenwriter: **Satyajit Ray**, from a story by Tarashankar Banerjee. Cinematographer: Soumendu Roy. Art director: Bansi Chandragupta. Music: **Satyajit Ray**. Editor: Dulal Dutta. 150 min.
Principal Cast: Soumitra Chatterjee (Narsingh), Waheeda Rehman (Gulabi), Ruma Guha Thakurta (Neeli), Gyanesh Mukherjee (Josef), Charuprakash Ghosh (Sukhanram), Robi Ghosh (Rama), Shekhar Chatterjee (Rameshwar), Reba Devi (Joseph's mother)

Mahanagar (*The Big City*) (1963)
Director: **Satyajit Ray**. Production company: R. D. Bansal & Co. Producer: R. D. Bansal. Screenwriter: **Satyajit Ray**, from a story by Narendranath Mitra. Cinematographer: Subrata Mitra. Art director: Bansi Chandragupta. Music: Satyajit Ray. Editor: Dulal Dutta. 131 min.
Principal Cast: Anil Chatterjee (Subrata Mazumdar), Madhabi Mukherjee (Arati Mazumdar), Jaya Bhaduri (Bani), Haren Chatterjee (Priyogopal), Sefalika Devi (Sarojini), Prasenjit Sarkar (Pintu), Haradhan Bannerjee (Himangshu Mukherjee), Vicky Redwood (Edith)

FILMOGRAPHY

Charulata (*The Lonely Wife*) (1964)

Director: **Satyajit Ray**. Production company: R. D. Bansal & Co. Producer: R. D. Bansal. Screenwriter: **Satyajit Ray**, from a story by Rabindranath Tagore. Cinematographer: Subrata Mitra. Art director: Bansi Chandragupta. Music: **Satyajit Ray**. Editor: Dulal Dutta. 117 min.
Principal Cast: Madhabi Mukherjee (Charulata), Soumitra Chatterjee (Amal), Shailen Mukherjee (Bhupati Dutta)

Mahapurush (*The Holy Man*) (1965)

Director: **Satyajit Ray**. Production company: R. D. Bansal & Co. Producer: R. D. Bansal. Screenwriter: **Satyajit Ray**, from a story by Rajshekar "Parashuram" Basu. Cinematographer: Soumendu Roy. Art director: Bansi Chandragupta. Music: **Satyajit Ray**. Editor: Dulal Dutta. 65 min.
Principal Cast: Charuprakas Ghosh (Birinchi Baba), Robi Ghosh (Birinchi Baba's assistant) Prasad Mukherjee (Gurupada Mitter), Gitali Roy (Buchki), Satindra Bhattacharya (Satya), Somen Bose (Nibaran), Santosh Dutta (Professor Nani), Renuka Roy (Nani's wife), Satya Banerjee (Nitai), Haridhan Mukherjee (Ganesh)

Kapurush (*The Coward*) (1965)

Director: **Satyajit Ray**. Production company: R. D. Bansal & Co. Producer: R. D. Bansal. Screenwriter: **Satyajit Ray**, from a story by Premendra Mitra. Cinematographer: Soumendu Roy. Art director: Bansi Chandragupta. Music: **Satyajit Ray**. Editor: Dulal Dutta. 74 min.

Principal Cast: Soumitra Chatterjee (Amitabha Roy), Madhabi Mukherjee (Karuna Gupta), Haridhan Bannerjee (Bimal Gupta)

Two: A Film Fable (also known as *Parable of the Two*)
(TV short) (1965)
Director: **Satyajit Ray**. Production company: Esso World Theatre (PBS). Screenwriter: **Satyajit Ray**. Cinematographer: Soumendu Roy. Art director: Bansi Chandragupta. Music: **Satyajit Ray**. 12 min.
Cast: Ravi Kiran, uncredited boy.

Shakespeare-Wallah (1965)
Director: James Ivory. Production company: Merchant Ivory Productions. Producer: Ismail Merchant. Screenwriter: James Ivory, Ruth Prawer Jhabvala. Cinematographer: Subrata Mitra. Music: **Satyajit Ray**. Editor: Amit Bose. 120 min.
Principal Cast: Shashi Kapoor (Sanju), Felicity Kendal (Lizzie Buckingham), Geoffrey Kendal (Tony Buckingham), Laura Liddell (Carla Buckingham), Madhur Jaffrey (Manjula), Utpal Dutt (Maharaja), Praveen Paul (Didi), Prayag Raj (Sharmaji), Pinchoo Kapoor (Guptaji), Jim T. Tytler (Bobby), Hamid Sayani (headmaster's brother), Marcus Murch (Dandy), Partap Sharma (Aslam)

Nayak (*Nayak: The Hero*) (1966)
Director: **Satyajit Ray**. Production company: R. D. Bansal & Co. Producer: R. D. Bansal. Screenwriter: **Satyajit Ray**, from a story by Premendra Mitra. Cinematographer: Subrata Mitra.

Art director: Bansi Chandragupta. Music: **Satyajit Ray**. Editor: Dulal Dutta, **Satyajit Ray**. 120 min.

Principal Cast: Uttam Kumar (Arindam Mukherjee), Sharmila Tagore (Aditi), Bireswar Sen (Mukanda Lahiri), Somen Bose (Sankar), Nirmal Ghosh (Jyoti), Premangshu Bose (Biresh), Sumita Sanyal (Promila Chatterjee), Ranjit Sen (Haren Bose), Bharati Devi (Manorama), Lali Chowdhury (Bulbul), Kamu Mukherjee (Pritish Sarkar), Susmita Mukherjee (Molly), Subrata Sensharma (Ajoy), Jamuna Sinha (Sefalika), Hiralal (Kamal Misra)

Chiriyakhana (*The Zoo*) (1967)

Director: **Satyajit Ray**. Production company: Star Productions. Producer: Harendraneth Bhattachayra. Screenwriter: **Satyajit Ray**, from a novel by Saradindu Bandopaddhyay. Cinematographer: Soumendu Roy. Art director: Bansi Chandragupta. Music: **Satyajit Ray**. Editor: Dulal Dutta. 125 min.

Principal Cast: Uttam Kumar (Satyanweshi Byomkesh)

Goopy Gyne Bagha Byne
(*The Adventures of Goopy and Bagha*) (1969)

Director: **Satyajit Ray**. Production company: Purnima Pictures. Producer: Asim Dutta, Nepal Dutta. Screenwriter: **Satyajit Ray**, from a story by Kishore Raychowdhuri. Cinematographer: Soumendu Roy. Art director: Bansi Chandragupta. Music: **Satyajit Ray**. Editor: Dulal Dutta. 132 min.

Principal Cast: Tapan Chatterjee (Goopy), Robi Ghosh (Bagha)

FILMOGRAPHY

Aranyer Din Ratri (*Days and Nights in the Forest*) (1970)
Director: **Satyajit Ray**. Production company: Priya Films.
Producer: Asim Dutta, Nepal Dutta. Screenwriter: **Satyajit Ray**, from a story by Sunil Gangopadhyay. Cinematographer: Soumendu Roy. Art director: Bansi Chandragupta. Music: **Satyajit Ray**. Editor: Dulal Dutta. 115 min.
Principal Cast: Sharmila Tagore (Aparna), Kaberi Bose (Jaya), Simi Garewal (Duli), Soumitra Chatterjee (Ashim), Subhendu Chatterjee (Sanjoy), Robi Ghosh (Shekhar), Samit Bhanja (Hari), Pahadi Sanyal (Sadashiv Tripathi), Premashish Sen

Pratidwandi (*The Adversary*, also known as *Siddharta and the City*) (1970)
Director: **Satyajit Ray**. Production company: Priya Films.
Producer: Asim Dutta, Nepal Dutta. Screenwriter: **Satyajit Ray**, from a story by Sunil Gangopadhyay. Cinematographer: Pernendu Bose, Soumendu Roy. Art director: Bansi Chandragupta. Music: **Satyajit Ray**. Editor: Dulal Dutta. 110 min.
Principal Cast: Dhritiman Chatterjee (Siddhartha Chaudhuri)

Baksa Badal (1970)
Director: Nityananda Datta. Production company: D. M. Productions. Producer: Nripan Gangopadhyay, Durgadas Mitra. Screenwriter: **Satyajit Ray**, from a story by Bibhutibhushan Bandyopadhyay. Cinematographer: Soumendu Roy. Art director: Bansi Chandragupta. Music: **Satyajit Ray**. Editor: Ramesh Joshi. 105 min.

Principal Cast: Soumitra Chatterjee (Dr. Pratul Bhattacharjee), Aparna Sen (Minu)

Seemabaddha (*Company Limited*) (1971)

Director: **Satyajit Ray**. Producer: Barat Shumsher, Jung Bahadur Rama. Screenwriter: **Satyajit Ray**, from a novel by Manisankar "Sankar" Mukherjee. Cinematographer: Soumendu Roy. Art director: Ashoke Bose. Music: **Satyajit Ray**. Editor: Dulal Dutta. 110 min.

Principal Cast: Sharmila Tagore (Tutul), Barun Chandra (Shyamalendu Chatterjee), Paromiter Chowdhury (Dolan)

Sikkem (documentary) (1971)

Director: **Satyajit Ray**. Producer: The Chogyal of Sikkem. Screenwriter: **Satyajit Ray**. Cinematographer: Soumendu Roy. Music: **Satyajit Ray**. Editor: Dulal Dutta. 55 min.

Principal Cast: **Satyajit Ray** (narrator)

The Inner Eye (documentary) (1972)

Director: **Satyajit Ray**. Production company: Films Division, Government of India. Screenwriter: **Satyajit Ray**. Cinematographer: Soumendu Roy. Music: **Satyajit Ray**. Editor: Dulal Dutta. 20 min.

Principal Cast: Binode Bihari Mukherjee (himself), **Satyajit Ray** (narrator)

Asani Sanket (1973)

Director: **Satyajit Ray**. Production company: Balaka Movies. Producer: Sharbani Bhattachayra. Screenwriter: **Satyajit**

Ray, from a story by Bibhutibhushan Bandyopadhyay.
Cinematographer: Soumendu Roy. Art director: Ashoke Bose.
Music: **Satyajit Ray**. Editor: Dulal Dutta. 101 min.
Principal Cast: Soumitra Chatterjee (Gangacharan
Chakravarti), Bobita (Ananga), Sandhya Roy (Chutki)

Sonar Kella (The Golden Fortress) (1974)

Director: **Satyajit Ray**. Production company: Government of
West Bengal. Screenwriter: **Satyajit Ray**. Cinematographer:
Soumendu Roy. Art director: Ashoke Bose. Music: **Satyajit
Ray**. Editor: Dulal Dutta. 120 min.
Principal Cast: Soumitra Chatterjee (Prodosh Mitra)

Jana Aranya (The Middleman) (1976)

Director: **Satyajit Ray**. Production company: Indus Films.
Producer: Subir Guha. Screenwriter: **Satyajit Ray**, from a
novel by Manisankar "Sankar" Mukherjee. Cinematographer:
Soumendu Roy. Art director: Ashoke Bose. Music: **Satyajit
Ray**. Editor: Dulal Dutta. 131 min.
Principal Cast: Pradip Mukherjee (Somnath)

Bala (documentary) (1976)

Director: **Satyajit Ray**. Production company: National Center
for Performing Arts, Bombay, Government of Tamil Nadu.
Screenwriter: **Satyajit Ray**. Cinematographer: Soumendu Roy.
Music: **Satyajit Ray**. Editor: Dulal Dutta. 31 min.
Principal Cast: Balasaraswati

FILMOGRAPHY

Shatranj Ke Khilari (The Chess Players) (1977)
Director: **Satyajit Ray**. Production company: Devki Chitra.
Producer: Suresh Jindal. Screenwriter: **Satyajit Ray**, from the
novel by Munshi Premchand. Cinematographer: Soumendu
Roy. Art director: Bansi Chandragupta. Music: **Satyajit Ray**.
Editor: Dulal Dutta. 129 min.
Principal Cast: Sanjeev Kumar (Mirza Sajjad Ali), Saeed Jaffrey
(Mir Roshan Ali), Shabana Azmi (Khurshid), Farida Jalal
(Nafisa), Veena (Queen Mother), David Abraham (Munshi),
Victor Banerjee (Prime Minister), Farooq Shaikh (Aqueel),
Tom Alter (Capt. Weston), Leela Mishra (Hirya), Samarth
Narain (Kallu), Bhudo Advani (Abbajani), Kamu Mukherjee,
Barry John, Uttamram Nagar

Joi Baba Felunath: The Elephant God (1979)
Director: **Satyajit Ray**. Production company: R. D. Bansal
& Co. Producer: R. D. Bansal. Screenwriter: **Satyajit Ray**.
Cinematographer: Soumendu Roy. Art director: Ashoke Bose.
Music: **Satyajit Ray**. Editor: Dulal Dutta. 112 min.
Principal Cast: Soumitra Chatterjee (Prodosh Mitra)

Heerak Rajar Deshe (Kingdom of Diamonds) (1980)
Director: **Satyajit Ray**. Production company: Government of
West Bengal. Screenwriter: **Satyajit Ray**. Cinematographer:
Soumendu Roy. Art director: Ashoke Bose. Music: **Satyajit
Ray**. Editor: Dulal Dutta. 118 min.
Principal Cast: Soumitra Chatterjee (Pondit Moshai), Utpal Dutt
(Hirak Raja), Robi Ghosh (Bagha Bayen), Tapan Chatterjee
(Goopy Gayen), Santosh Dutta (King of Shundi/ scientist)

FILMOGRAPHY

Sadgati (*Deliverance*) (TV movie) (1981)

Director: **Satyajit Ray**. Production company: Doordarshan, Government of India (Indian National Television). Screenwriter: **Satyajit Ray**, based on a story by Munshi Premchand. Cinematographer: Soumendu Roy. Art director: Ashoke Bose. Music: **Satyajit Ray**. Editor: Dulal Dutta. 52 min.

Principal Cast: Om Puri (Dukhi Chamar), Smita Patil (Jhuria), Mohan Agashe (Ghashiram, the Brahmin), Gita Siddharth (Lakshmi), Richa Mishra (Dhania), Salil Dhar Diwan, Shyam Sundar Sharma, Wahid Shareef, Anand Chaube, Anand Verma, Narendra Thakak

Pikoo (*Pikoo's Diary*) (TV short) (1981)

Director: **Satyajit Ray**. Production company: France 3. Producer: Henri Fraise. Screenwriter: **Satyajit Ray**. Cinematographer: Soumendu Roy. Music: **Satyajit Ray**. Editor: Dulal Dutta. 26 min.

Principal Cast: Victor Bannerjee (the lover), Arjan Guha-Thakurta (Pikoo), Soven Lahiri (Pikoo's grandfather), Aparna Sen (Pikoo's mother)

Phatik Chand (1983)

Director: Sandip Ray. Production company: France 3. Producer: Bimal Kumar Gupta. Screenwriter: **Satyajit Ray**. Cinematographer: Soumendu Roy. Music: **Satyajit Ray**. Editor: Dulal Dutta. 103 min.

Principal Cast: Haradhan Bannerjee (Fatik's father), Biplab Chatterjee (Shyam Lal), Tarun Mitra, Ramesh Mukherjee, Kamal Deb, Bhishma Guhathakurta, Ashok Mukherjee,

Kaushik Banerjee, Kartik Chatterjee, Sunil Gupta Kabiraj, Nirmal Mitra, Ashok Das, Sunil Sarkar

Ghare-Baire (*The Home and the World*) (1984)
Director: **Satyajit Ray**. Production company: National Film Development Corporation of India (NFDC). Screenwriter: **Satyajit Ray**, from the novel by Rabindranath Tagore. Cinematographer: Soumendu Roy. Art director: Ashoke Bose. Music: **Satyajit Ray**. Editor: Dulal Dutta. 140 min.
Principal Cast: Soumitra Chatterjee (Sandip Mukherjee), Victor Banerjee (Nikhilesh Choudhury), Swatilekha Sengupta (Bimala Choudhury), Gopa Aich (sister-in-law), Jennifer Kendal (Miss Gilby), Manoj Mitra (headmaster), Bimala Chatterjee (Kulada), Indrapramit Roy (Amulya)

Sukumar Ray (documentary) (1987)
Director: **Satyajit Ray**. Production company: Government of West Bengal. Screenwriter: **Satyajit Ray**. Cinematographer: Barun Raha. Art director: Ashoke Bose. Music: **Satyajit Ray**. Editor: Dulal Dutta. 26 min.
Principal Cast: Soumitra Chatterjee, Utpal Dutt

Ganashatru (*An Enemy of the People*) (1989)
Director: **Satyajit Ray**. Production company: National Film Development Corporation of India (NDFC). Producer: Ravi Malik. Screenwriter: **Satyajit Ray**, from the play by Henrik Ibsen. Cinematographer: Barun Raha. Art director: Ashoke Bose. Music: **Satyajit Ray**. Editor: Dulal Dutta. 99 min.

Principal Cast: Soumitra Chatterjee (Dr. Ashok Gupta), Dhritiman Chatterjee (Nishith Gupta), Dipankar Dey (Haridas Bagchi), Ruma Guha Thakurta (Maya Gupta), Mamata Shankar (Indrani Gupta), Subhendu Chatterjee (Biresh Guha), Bhishma Guhathakurta (Ranen Halder), Satya Bannerjee (landlord), Rajoram Yaknig (Mr. Barghav)

Shahka Proshakha (Branches of the Tree) (1990)
Director: **Satyajit Ray**. Production company: Satyajit Ray Productions, DD Productions, Distri Films, Erato Films, Sopro Films. Producer: Gérard Depardieu, Daniel Toscan du Plantier. Screenwriter: **Satyajit Ray**. Cinematographer: Barun Raha. Art director: Ashoke Bose. Music: **Satyajit Ray**. Editor: Dulal Dutta. 130 min.
Principal Cast: Ajit Banerjee (Ananda Majumdar), Haradhan Bannerjee (Probodh), Soumitra Chatterjee (Prasahnto), Dipankar Dey (Probir), Ranjit Mallick (Protap), Lily Chakravarty (Uma), Mamata Shankar (Tapati)

Agantuk (The Stranger) (1991)
Director: **Satyajit Ray**. Production company: National Film Development Corporation of India (NDFC), Canal+, DD Productions, Erato Films. Producer: **Satyajit Ray**, Gérard Depardieu, Daniel Toscan du Plantier. Screenwriter: **Satyajit Ray**. Cinematographer: Barun Raha. Ashoke Bose. Music: **Satyajit Ray**. Editor: Dulal Dutta. 120 min.
Principal Cast: Dipankar Dey (Sudhindra Bose), Mamata Shankar (Anila Bose), Bikram Bhattacharya (Satyaki Bose), Utpal Dutt (Manomohan Mitra), Dhritiman Chatterjee

(Prithwish Sen Gupta), Robi Ghosh (Ranjan Rakshit), Subrata Chatterjee (Chhanda Rakshit), Promode Ganguly (Tridib Mukherjee), Ajit Banerjee (Sital Sarkar)

Goopy Bagha Phire Elo (1991)

Director: Sandip Ray. Production company: Government of West Bengal. Screenwriter: Sandip Ray, from a story by **Satyajit Ray**. Cinematographer: Barun Raha. Art Director: Ashoke Bose. Music: **Satyajit Ray**. Editor: Dulal Dutta. 119 min.

Principal Cast: Robi Ghosh (Bagha), Tapan Chatterjee (Goopy), Ajit Banerjee (Bhrahmananda Acharya).

Uttoran (The Broken Journey) (1994)

Director: Sandip Ray. Production company: Doordarshan, Filmopolis, National Film Development Corporation of India (NDFC). Screenwriter: **Satyajit Ray**. Cinematographer: Barun Raha. Art director: Ashoke Dutt. Music: Sandip Ray. Editor: Dulal Dutta. 90 min.

Principal Cast: Soumitra Chatterjee (Dr. Sengupta), Debatosh Ghosh (Haladhar), Sadhu Meher (Jatin Kundu), Suvalakshmi (Manashi), Bina, Lily Chakravarty, Mirakshi Goswani

INDEX

A bout de souffle. See *Breathless*
Antonioni, Michelangelo, 7, 12
Avventura, L', 7

Bannerjee, Bibhuti Bhushan, 17
Bergman, Ingmar, vii, x, xi, xiii, xvii, 1, 3, 12, 53
Bicycle Thieves, 3
Big Sky, The, 93
Birds, The, 48
Bonnes Femmes, Les, 7
Breathless, 7
Bresson, Robert, 110
Broken Blossoms, 7, 8

Capra, Frank, 3
Charulata, 2, 7, 14, 16, 79
Chatterjee, Soumitra, 15, 56–57, 80–81, 107
Citizen Kane, 7

Days and Nights in the Forest, xvii, 14, 15–16, 17, 44, 79, 80, 122
De Sica, Vittorio, 3

Devi, 3, 6, 54, 80

Edwards, Blake, xvii
Europa '51, 94–95, 110

Ford, John, 3, 7

Ghoshal, Sumarin, 56
Godard, Jean-Luc, 1–2, 7, 12
Griffith, D. W., 8
Gupta, Pinaki Sen, 56

Hawks, Howard, vii, viii, x, xvii, 7, 88, 93
Hitchcock, Alfred, vii, x, xii, xvii, 3, 12, 48

Kaul, Goutam, 6

Lawrence, D. H., 22–23, 90
Losey, Joseph, 82

*M*A*S*H*, 82
Mahanagar, 2, 12–13

INDEX

Mizoguchi, Kenji, 7, 8
Mozart, Wolfgang Amadeus, 14, 16
Murnau, F. W., 96
Music Room, The (Jalsaghar), xvi, 79

Party, The, xvii
Passage to India (novel), 30
Penn, Arthur, vii, x, xvii
Pericles (Shakespeare), 111
Philosopher's Stone, The, xvi, 79
Polanski, Roman, 82
Powys, T. F., x, 82
Prise de Pouvoir par Louis XIV, La, 110

Rainbow, The (Lawrence), 22–23
Red River, 88
Règle du jeu, La, 17
Renoir, Jean, xii, 3, 7, 8, 14–15, 16–18
River, The, 3, 16–18
Rossellini, Roberto, 88, 94–95, 109–10

Rules of the Game. See *Règle du jeu, La*

Sellers, Peter, xvii
Shakespeare, William, 111, 119
Shame (1968), xi
Silence, The, 53
Southerner, The, 3
Stromboli, 110
Sunrise, 95–96

Tagore, Rabindranath, 9
Two Daughters, 4, 9, 14, 54

Unclay (Powys), x, 82

Vaidyanathan, T. G., 5
Viaggio in Italia, 95, 110

Walker, Michael, 109
Winter's Tale, A (Shakespeare), 111, 119
Wordsworth, William, 48, 105